PREPARATORY COURSE FOR THE
ASWB BACHELORS LEVEL EXAM

Human Development, Diversity, and Behavior in the Environment

**Association for Advanced Training
in the Behavioral Sciences**
212 W. Ironwood Drive, Suite D #168 Coeur d'Alene, ID 83814
(800) 472-1931

© Association for Advanced Training in the Behavioral Sciences. All rights reserved. No part of these materials may be reproduced in any form, or by any means, mechanical or electronic, including photocopying, without the written permission of the publisher. To reproduce or adapt, in whole or in part, any portion of these materials is not only a violation of copyright law, but is unethical and unprofessional. As a condition of your acceptance of these materials, you agree not to reproduce or adapt them in any manner or license others to do so. The unauthorized resale of these materials is prohibited. The Association for Advanced Training in the Behavioral Sciences accepts the responsibility of protecting not only its own interests, but to protect the interests of its authors and to maintain and vigorously enforce all copyrights on its material. Your cooperation in complying with the copyright law is appreciated.

BACHELORS LEVEL

HUMAN DEVELOPMENT, DIVERSITY, AND BEHAVIOR IN THE ENVIRONMENT

Table of Contents

I. Theories and Models of Human Development and Behavior 1
   A. The Biopsychosocial Perspective 1
   B. Person-Environment Interactions 4
   C. General Systems Theory 9
   D. Psychodynamic Theories 11
   E. Erikson's Theory of Psychosocial Development 16
   F. Learning Theories 17
   G. Cognitive Theories 20
   H. Role Theory 21
   I. Social Psychology Research 23

II. Human Development Over the Lifespan 27
   A. Heredity and the Environment 27
   B. Physical Growth and Development 28
   C. Cognitive Growth and Development 40
   D. Language Development and Acquisition 44
   E. Temperament and Family Influences on Personality 47
   F. Identity Development 48
   G. Development of Self-Awareness and Self-Concept 50
   H. Attachment 53
   I. Communication 56
   J. Emotional Growth and Development 58
   K. Moral Development 63
   L. Social Growth and Development 64
   M. Sexual Growth and Development 69
   N. Spiritual Development 73

III. Family Theories and Dynamics 74
   A. Overview of "Family" 74
   B. Marriage 75
   C. Parenthood and Parenting 76

    D. Grandparenthood 81
    E. Divorce 81
    F. Remarriage, Stepparenting, and Blended Families 83
    G. Adoption 84
    H. Foster Care 87

IV. School and Worklife **91**
    A. School 91
    B. Worklife 93

V. Group Theory and Dynamics **96**

VI. Community Functioning and Development **99**
    A. Community Characteristics and Functions 99
    B. Community Concepts and Theories 100
    C. Power, Conflict, and Politics in Communities 105

VII. Understanding the Influence of Diversity **109**
    A. Prejudice, Discrimination, Oppression, and Racism 109
    B. Culture 111
    C. Sexual Orientation 115
    D. Gender 118
    E. Physical Disability 120
    F. Poverty and Homelessness 123
    G. Criminal Justice Systems 126

VIII. Social Policy **127**
    A. Evolution of Social Service Delivery in the U.S. 127
    B. Policies Affecting Social Service Delivery 129

BACHELORS LEVEL

HUMAN DEVELOPMENT, DIVERSITY, AND BEHAVIOR IN THE ENVIRONMENT

NOTE: The use of pronouns is extensive in our study material. To avoid cumbersome phrasing and simplify your reading, we use primarily masculine pronouns in some chapters and primarily feminine pronouns in others. In this chapter, we use primarily "he," "him," "his," etc. In other chapters, we use primarily "she," "her," etc.

In this chapter, we review the biophysical, psychological, and social factors that influence how human beings develop, mature, and change from conception through old age. Elsewhere in these materials, in the chapter on Assessment, we apply this information by describing how social workers derive and explore hypotheses about biophysical, psychological, and social factors to identify possible causes and explanations for their clients' functioning.

I. Theories and Models of Human Development and Behavior

A. The Biopsychosocial Perspective

Social workers have relied for many years on "person-in-environment (PIE) theory," a framework that emphasizes the importance of context: **PIE theory** assumes that human problems have their roots in both individual and situational factors and that understanding and treating human problems requires a dual focus on the individual and environmental forces. Social work's commitment to taking context into account provides the basis for the **biopsychosocial perspective**, which maintains that biophysical (biological), psychological, and social factors all play a significant role in human development and functioning.

Biopsychosocial Functioning

To understand what influences their clients' development and behavior, social workers adopt a multidimensional framework that focuses on the biophysical, psychological, and social dimensions. These interacting dimensions are conceptualized as a system of biopsychosocial functioning (Ashford et al., 2006):

- The **biophysical dimension** is concerned with all the biological and physiological factors that influence human development and behavior. It consists of biophysical growth and development from the prenatal period to old age, biophysical strengths (protective factors), and biophysical hazards (risks).

- The **psychological dimension** is concerned with psychological functions that influence a person's ability to satisfy his needs over the lifespan. It consists of early emotional bonding, basic temperament, cognitive development and information processing, communication, personality, identity, and self-concept, emotions and attitudes, social regulation, moral development, psychological strengths (protective factors), and psychological hazards (risks).

- The **social dimension** consists of family, social supports, and the various groups, communities, organizations, and social institutions (church, school, health-care providers, welfare services, etc.) that a person interacts with over his lifetime. It also includes gender and multicultural considerations, social strengths (protective factors), and social hazards (risks).

The related concept of "**biopsychosocial interaction**" assumes that no single factor is solely responsible for causing a person's behavioral responses. Instead, human behavior is the result of interactions between a person and his environment. At all levels (individual, family, group, organizational, community, societal), these interactions can be assessed using two perspectives: (a) A *developmental perspective* focuses on how biophysical, psychological, and social systems have interacted in leading up to how things are now; and (b) a *current perspective* examines how biophysical, psychological, and social systems are currently interacting to influence how things are now.

Human Needs

"Needs" are physical, psychological, economic, cultural, and social requirements for survival, fulfillment, and well-being and, therefore, encompass all dimensions of a person's life, including biophysical, psychological, and social. Items that are considered essential for the maintenance of a person's well-being, such as adequate food, clean water, shelter, clothing, heating, fuel, and security from bodily harm, are referred to as **basic needs**.

1. Categories of Needs: There are several ways of conceptualizing needs, including the following:

- *Normative needs* include what a person requires in order to attain a level of well-being that meets the established standards of his community or culture.

- *Perceived needs* include the requirements that individuals believe they must have in order to achieve an acceptable level of well-being.

- *Expressed need* is an indication of the degree to which a need exists and the number of people who perceive themselves to have that need, as demonstrated by specific factors such as how many people apply for a service.

- *Relative needs* describe the requirements that people must have met in order to attain an acceptable level of well-being as compared to other people's requirements. The term is often used when discussing gaps between needs and services or differences in the availability of services to different groups of people in need (Barker, 2003).

2. Basic Human Attachments: Some authors conceptualize critical human needs in terms of "basic human attachments." These attachments include the following: physical supplies necessary to life (e.g., oxygen, food); a sense of personal identity; a mutually supportive and close relationship with at least one other person; membership in at least one group that accepts us; one or more roles that promote a sense of self-respect and allow us to perform with dignity; financial security or a way of engaging in an exchange of the goods and services we need and value; and a system of meaning or set of values that helps us determine our goals and understand ourselves and the world.

3. Maslow's Needs Hierarchy: Abraham Maslow's needs hierarchy can be used to rank and evaluate the needs of individuals (or communities) and assess the adequacy of services. Maslow's framework moves from the lowest level of basic survival needs up to the highest level of self-actualization needs:

- Survival and physiological needs – food, clothing, shelter, medical care.
- Safety and security needs – protection from harm and violence.
- Social (belonging) needs – opportunity to interact in a positive environment.
- Esteem (ego) needs – opportunity to build self-respect and achieve personal dignity.
- Self-actualization needs – opportunity for lifelong education and self-improvement.

According to Maslow, lower-level needs must be addressed before an individual can move to the next level. If a lower-level need is not being met, the person moves back down the hierarchy to satisfy that unmet need.

Risk and Resilience

The biopsychosocial perspective is concerned with the balance of risks and protective factors that interact to determine a person's tendency toward resilience.

1. Risks, Protective Factors, and Resilience: A variety of biophysical, psychological, and social hazards ("risks") and strengths ("protective factors") affect a person's development and behavior over the lifespan. **Risks** are hazards in the person or environment that increase the likelihood of a problem occurring. Examples of risks include a genetic predisposition for a mental disorder, insecure attachment pattern, and living in poverty. **Protective factors** that coexist with risks are personal, social, and institutional factors that promote personal competence and successful development and, therefore, decrease the likelihood of a problem occurring. Examples of protective factors include adequate prenatal care, active coping mechanisms, and low family stress. In turn, **resilience** refers to a person's ability to function adaptively despite exposure to risks.

2. Family Risk Factors: Rutter (1985) argues that the greater the number of risk factors a baby is exposed to, the greater the risk for negative outcomes. He concluded that the following family risk factors – known as **Rutter's indicators** – are particularly accurate predictors of child psychopathology: (a) severe marital discord, (b) low socioeconomic status (SES), (c) overcrowding or large family size, (d) parental criminality, (e) maternal psychopathology, and (f) placement of the child outside the home.

3. Studies on Risk and Resilience: A number of studies have been conducted in an effort to identify why some children do well despite facing many biophysical, psychological, and/or social risks. Werner and Smith (1982; Werner, 1993) found that positive outcomes for high-risk babies are more likely when they: (a) experience fewer stressors following birth (e.g., more negative effects are associated with chronic poverty, family instability, and maternal health problems); (b) have an easy temperament characterized by a high degree of social responsivity, good communication skills, and consistent eating and sleeping patterns; and (c) are provided with stable support from a parent or other caregiver. These findings suggest that high-risk children can demonstrate resilience and that the negative effects of prenatal and perinatal stress are not always irreversible.

Other investigators have identified characteristics of an adolescent and his environment that contribute to positive outcomes despite facing risks. Factors contributing to adolescent stress resistance include (a) positive and nurturant relationships with others (including his parents), (b) an easy temperament and positive outlook on the future, (c) an internal locus of control and good self-regulation, (d) an active coping style, (e) good social skills and social support, (f) good cognitive skills (problem-solving abilities) and intellectual abilities, and (g) outside activities and hobbies (Masten, 2001; Masten & Coatsworth, 1998).

The Strengths Perspective

The strengths perspective defines a **strength** is anything positive that a person is doing, can do, or wants to do (Sheafor & Horejsi, 2003). Specific strengths found in an individual or group may consist of ability, energy, courage, knowledge, experience, fortitude, goodwill, integrity, etc.

The assumptions and principles of the strengths perspective include the following:

- Every person, family, group, and community has strengths, and it is the social worker's responsibility to identify a client's strengths and build on them.
- Every neighborhood and community has helpful resources that are available and can be mobilized if an individual is creative and persistent.
- No one can know the full extent of a person's capacity to grow, change, and overcome problems.
- Negative and traumatic events can injure and impose limitations on a person, but they can also be sources of challenge and opportunity.
- It is usually easier to help a person achieve positive and lasting change by building on his strengths than by trying to eliminate his problems or deficiencies.
- A person generally knows what will and will not be effective and helpful in addressing his problems and concerns. A social worker should collaborate with a client and take seriously the client's goals and suggestions.

B. Person-Environment Interactions

When applying the concept of **person-in-environment** (or "person-in-situation"), social workers are concerned with the interaction between a person and his environment. Key systems involved in person-environment interactions include individual (biophysical, cognitive, emotional, behavioral, motivational); interpersonal (marital, family, friends, cultural groups, etc.); communal/societal (community, organizations, institutions); and the physical environment itself (housing, climate, etc.).

The Capacity for Adaptation

Human behavior occurs in a wide range of contexts in which people face ongoing biophysical, psychological, and social demands that require them to respond in effective ways. The ability to respond effectively to these demands is known as **adaptation**, and the capacity to adapt and succeed within a changing environment is related to a person's capacity for "developmental flexibility" (Mahoney, 2000). Social workers recognize that a person's capacity for adaptation can be improved by enhancing his behavioral competence in adapting to biophysical, psychological, and social demands or by enhancing his environment.

Ecological Systems (Ecosystems) Perspective

The **ecosystems perspective**, which combines systems theory and concepts associated with ecology, assumes that human development must be seen within the context of an individual's relationship with his environment and that each environment is unique. Germain, who was instrumental in applying ecosystems concepts to social work, advocated a "transactional" view of the person-environment relationship, which proposes that a person and his environment engage in ongoing circular exchanges in which they reciprocally influence each other over time.

1. Key Ecology Terms and Concepts: "Ecology" is the study of the relationship between an organism and its biological and physical environments, including how the organism adapts and functions in these environments. In turn, an **ecosystem** (the unit of study in ecology) is "a partially or completely self-contained mass of organisms ... [that engages in] interactions and material cycling that link the organisms in a community with one another and their environment" (Sheafor & Horejsi, 2003, p. 91). Two important concepts associated with ecology are adaptation and competition:

- Because ecosystems are always changing, each species (whether plant, animal, or human) in an ecosystem is constantly adapting to an environment that continues to change: If the environment changes rapidly or the species can't adapt quickly enough, the species may be overpowered or replaced by a more adaptable species.

- Because resources (e.g., food, water, space) are usually limited, the various species in an ecosystem must compete in order to survive. When resources needed by a particular species are scarce, the individual members of that species must also compete with each other. Therefore, competition plays a major role in shaping ecological communities. Competition can lead to a higher level of functioning but also can be destructive.

2. Ecological Concepts Applied to Humans: Ecological concepts are transactional in nature – they express a relationship rather than referring to either person or environment alone.

a. Adaptedness: A central concept in ecology is state of **adaptedness**, which refers to a person's "**goodness of fit**" with his environment. This encompasses the adaptive balance of a person's needs, capacities, and goals with his social and physical environment, all within a particular culture and time.

- "Adaptive processes" are active efforts made by a person to bring about either (a) physiological and psychological changes in himself to fit the demands and opportunities of his environment or (b) changes in his environment so that his environment will be more favorable to his needs, rights, and goals.

- Because any change requires further adaptation, adaptation is a continuous process. It requires a reciprocal (back and forth) shaping of the person and environment over time and is, therefore, transactional in nature.

- When person-environment transactions are adaptive, a person's growth and development are supported by elements of his environment, which leads to further growth. When person-environment transactions are maladaptive, the opposite occurs.

- For humans, competition can lead to social and economic injustice and the oppression of some groups. When an individual can't make effective adaptations to changes in himself, other people, and/or the wider society, he experiences distress and is disadvantaged in his ability to compete.

b. Stress: From an ecological perspective, **stress** expresses a relationship between a person and his environment.

- Stress encompasses both (a) an environmental demand and (b) a person's subjective experience of physiological and psychological stress in response to the demand.

- Stress results in either a positive or negative person-environment relationship: (a) The relationship is positive when the person perceives an environmental demand as a challenge. "Positive stress" is associated with positive feelings. (b) The relationship is negative when there is a discrepancy between an actual or perceived environmental demand and the person's actual or perceived capacity to cope with it. "Negative stress" is associated with negative feelings (e.g., anxiety, guilt, rage, helplessness, low self-esteem).

c. Coping: Coping is the physiological, psychological, and behavioral response set in motion as a result of stress.

- The major functions of coping are problem-solving, dealing with negative feelings, and maintaining self-esteem. Because coping functions are interdependent and require both personal and environmental resources, they are a good indication of the status of person-environment relationship.

- Effective coping responses lead to the elimination of stress. If coping responses are ineffective, stress persists and can lead to physical, emotional, or social dysfunction, or all three.

d. Relatedness, Competence, Self-Direction, Identity, and Self-Esteem: These five concepts are all transactional in nature and, therefore, facilitate a focus on the person-environment relationship.

- *Human relatedness* is a biological and social imperative over the lifespan. It incorporates ideas about social and emotional loneliness and isolation. For example, people facing stress have been found to suffer less physical, emotional, and social dysfunction when they are surrounded by a supportive social network.

- *Competence* (sense of personal efficacy) can begin to develop right after birth if the infant experiences successful efforts at making his caregivers respond to his needs. For competence to continue developing, the social and physical environment must provide the person with diverse stimuli, learning opportunities, and support for age-appropriate exploration and self-direction throughout his life.

- Relatedness and competence, in turn, influence the development of *self-direction*, or the relative autonomy of the ego from external and internal pressures. Although autonomous, the ego remains attuned to internal and external needs. The concept of autonomy also takes into account issues of power, oppression, and the individual's location in the social structure.

- *Identity* and *self-esteem* arise from relationships with other people. Because evaluations made by others affect self-concept, a person's identity is reworked throughout life as a result of his interactions with his social and physical environment.

e. Niche and Habitat: Organisms, including humans, can adapt to and will function better in some environments (i.e., settings or contexts) than in others.

- The concept of **niche** refers to the particular combination of conditions and circumstances (e.g., temperature, soil, chemistry) needed by a particular species. For humans, niche includes the status occupied by a person or group within a given social structure and is related to issues of power and oppression. Generally, a person's niche is shaped by a set of rights, including the right to equal opportunity. However, in many communities, because of race, ethnicity, gender, age, sexual orientation, disability, poverty, or other personal or social characteristics devalued by some segments of society, many people are forced to occupy niches that are incongruent with their needs and goals.

- **Habitats** are the settings where an organism is found. In the case of humans, physical settings include dwellings, buildings, rural villages, and urban layouts. These habitats should support the social settings of family life, social life, work life, religious life, etc., in ways that suit the lifestyle, gender, age, and culture of individuals. Habitats that don't support these functions produce feelings of isolation and despair, which further interfere with the adaptive functioning of family and community life.

3. Key Ecosystems Perspective Principles: Based on the above concepts and concepts drawn from systems theory (which is reviewed a bit later in this section), the ecosystems perspective emphasizes the following principles:

- Because humans and environments mutually affect each other, human problems can be understood only when they're viewed in their environmental context. Human problems and their environmental settings are considered to constitute one system – the **problem system**. Every problem system is unique because its subsystems have different interactions and characteristics.

- Psychological processes are manifestations of interactions between and among biophysical, interpersonal, cultural, political, economic, legal, and organizational forces, and these forces interact continually and influence a person's behavior during his entire lifespan.

- To fulfill their needs and accomplish important developmental tasks, human beings must have adequate environmental resources and experience positive transactions with their environments. Humans experience stress and impaired functioning when their needs are not met. To reduce stress, coping efforts to fulfill unmet needs must take place. The ultimate goal of coping efforts is to achieve an adaptive person-environment fit.

- Human beings may lack effective coping strategies, adequate resources, or both. In social work, the objective is to help people find ways of meeting their needs by addressing those deficits. This involves (a) connecting a person to (or creating) needed resources and/or (b) improving the person's capacity to use resources or cope with negative environmental influences.

Bronfenbrenner's Ecological Model

Bronfenbrenner (2004) described development as involving interactions between the individual and his context or environment, and his ecological model describes the context in terms of five environmental systems or levels: The **microsystem** is the child's immediate environment and includes face-to-face relationships within the home, school, and neighborhood (e.g., the child's relationships with parents, siblings, peers, and teachers). The **mesosystem** refers to interactions between components of the microsystem, such as the influence of family factors on the child's behavior at school. The **exosystem** consists of elements in the broader environment that affect the child's immediate environment and includes the parents' workplace, the school board, community agencies, local industry, and the mass media. The **macrosystem** is comprised of such overarching environmental influences as cultural beliefs and practices, economic conditions, and political ideologies. Finally, the **chronosystem** consists of environmental events that occur over an individual's lifespan and impact the individual in ways that depend on the individual's circumstances and developmental stage (e.g., the immediate and long-term effects of a change in family structure or socioeconomic status).

Lewin's Field Theory

One of the first social psychologists to stress the importance of recognizing the influence of the environment on individual behavior was Kurt Lewin (1936). His recognition of the importance of the environment is reflected in his field theory, which proposes that "every psychological event depends on the state of the person and at the same time on the environment, although their relative importance is different in different cases" (p. 12). In other words, according to Lewin, human behavior is always a function of the person and the physical and social environment; i.e., $B = f(P, E)$.

Lewin applied field theory to a number of intra- and interpersonal phenomena including leadership, group dynamics, and conflict. With regard to conflict, Lewin (1931) distinguished between three types of intraindividual (motivational) conflict, and Miller (1944) subsequently added a fourth:

- An **approach-approach conflict** occurs when we must choose between two equally positive or attractive goals (e.g., two equally desirable jobs). The approach-approach conflict is usually the easiest one to resolve.

- An **avoidance-avoidance conflict** occurs when we must choose between two equally negative or unattractive goals (e.g., choosing between being laid off or accepting a lower-paid job in the company). An avoidance-avoidance conflict is difficult to resolve and can lead to indecision, inaction, or removing oneself from the situation.

- An **approach-avoidance conflict** (also known as a single approach-avoidance conflict) occurs when a single goal has both positive and negative qualities (e.g., deciding whether or not to accept a promotion that comes with an increase in salary but also an increase in job-related stress). In this situation, when we move closer to the goal (the decision to accept the job), the avoidance force becomes stronger; and, conversely, when we move farther away from the goal (the decision to refuse the job), the approach force increases.

- A **double approach-avoidance conflict** occurs when we have to choose between two goals that both have positive and negative qualities (e.g., choosing between two graduate schools that have both pros and cons). This type of conflict produces vacillation between the two alternatives and is usually the most difficult type of conflict to resolve.

C. General Systems Theory

General systems theory (or systems theory) was first described by the biologist Ludwig von Bertalanffy who came to believe that change might occur as the result of an interaction of parts of an organism. He was interested in looking at a system as a whole, with its relationships and interactions with other systems as a mechanism of growth and change. This perspective represented a departure from older theories that emphasized understanding the whole by breaking it into parts.

1. Underlying Concepts: Core concepts underlying general systems theory are defined below.

a. System: A **system** is a collection of interconnected and interrelated parts that form a distinct, organized, and functioning whole.

- Each system is part of a suprasystem. For example, a family system is part of a community system.
- A system is comprised of many parts, which are called **subsystems**. In a family system, for example, the parts may include the spousal subsystem, the parent-child subsystem, and the sibling subsystem.
- Each part of a system (each subsystem) is affected to some degree by all the other parts, and a change in one part of a system will have an effect on all other parts.

b. Boundary: Every system has a structural limitation that separates it from other systems, gives the system definition, and makes the system unique. This property is referred to as the **boundary**. The boundary of a social system (such as a family) defines who belongs to the system and who doesn't. Membership in the same system can differ from situation to situation.

Some boundaries are "thick" and others are permeable.

- Permeable boundaries allow energy or information to pass through. The more permeable the boundary, the more interaction the system has with its environment.
- A system grows by exchanging energy with its environment, and this exchange is possible only when the system's boundary is permeable.

c. Closed System: All biological and social systems are open systems, but systems vary in their degree of openness. A **closed system** has a nonpermeable (thick) boundary: It is isolated from its environment and highly resistant to influence by outside forces. A closed (noninteracting) system is usually considered to be dysfunctional.

d. Open System: An **open system** has a permeable (thin) boundary that allows an ongoing exchange of energy (information) with its environment. In other words, an open system continuously receives energy from and discharges energy to its environment. A relatively open (interacting) system is usually considered to be functional.

- Compared to a closed system, an open system is more adaptable and open to change. A system with an overly permeable boundary, however, is so easily influenced by forces outside the system that it is unstable and easily destroyed.

- An open system is constantly changing as a result of its ongoing interactions with the environment. Change doesn't necessarily lead to a problem, however: When a system is functioning properly, it is able to achieve a dynamic equilibrium with its environment. (See homeostasis, below.)

e. Entropy: Negentropy (negative entropy) refers to forces that maintain a system's organization and promote its development. When an open system closes in an effort to protect itself, an imbalance in the flow of energy between the system and its environment develops, in which the system sends out more energy than it brings in. This can lead to a state of disorganization known as **entropy**.

f. System Functioning: System functioning consists of four interrelated activities:

Input: The system takes in needed energy (information) from its environment.

Conversion Operations: The system processes transforming input so that it can use the input to sustain its functioning.

Output: The system interacts with other systems.

Feedback: The system monitors its own functioning and makes needed adjustments (varies its outputs and inputs) in order to maintain a steady state (see homeostasis, below). This is the primary means of control a system has in its interactions with its environment.

g. Homeostasis: The term **homeostasis** addresses the tendency for any system to react toward restoring the status quo in the event of change. In other words, a system tends to act in ways that allow it to maintain a steady state. "Steady" doesn't mean constant or unchanging. Instead, it refers to a sense of balance between the system and its environment. The term "calibration" describes the regulation of a system similar to setting a thermostat on a furnace.

h. Feedback: The balance or homeostasis of a system is maintained by **negative feedback**. When the "temperature" rises or falls out of the comfort range in a family system, for example, negative feedback recalibrates the system (reduces deviation) and restores a comfortable balance. For example, a mother's disapproving glance may be used to bring her unruly child back under control.

Positive feedback, by contrast, upsets the existing homeostatic balance and amplifies deviation from a steady state. Many techniques used in family therapy might be called positive feedback since they are designed to unbalance a family system's existing homeostasis and permit a more functional balance to emerge.

i. Equifinality and Multifinality: The principle of equifinality (same end) refers to the fact that a single effect or outcome may result from several different causes. The principle of multifinality (many ends) refers to the fact that one cause (one action) may produce many different effects or outcomes.

j. Interface: The term **interface** refers to the intersection or overlap of two or more systems, such as a family and a school. Social workers often engage in boundary work, which is work at the "interface" of two more systems to improve the interactions between the client system and relevant systems in a client's environment.

2. Application of Systems Theory to Social Systems: Examples of social systems include families, groups, communities, single organizations, and networks of affiliated organizations. When applied to social systems, systems theory acknowledges the importance of not only formal groups and organizations but also informal linkages. According to Warren (1978), a social system has the following characteristics:

- A social system is a structural organization of the interaction of units (parts) and endures over time.

- A social system has internal and external elements that relate the system to its environment and its units to each other.

- A social system can be distinguished from the environment around it because the system performs the function of boundary maintenance. Social systems must establish and maintain boundaries in order to survive; when their boundaries become blurred, social systems become less viable.

- A social system strives to maintain an equilibrium (homeostasis): It adapts to changes coming from outside the system so that it can minimize their impact on the system's organizational structure and regulate subsequent relationships.

D. Psychodynamic Theories

The various psychodynamic theories share several assumptions, including the following: (a) Human behavior is motivated largely by unconscious processes, (b) early development has a profound effect on adult functioning, and (c) universal principles explain personality development and behavior.

Freud's Personality Theory (Psychoanalytic Theory)

Sigmund Freud's personality theory consists of two separate, but interrelated, theories: a structural (drive) theory and a developmental theory.

1. Structural Theory: Freud's structural theory posits the personality with three structures – the id, the ego, and the superego.

a. The Id: The **id** is present at birth and consists of the person's life and death instincts, which serve as the source of all psychic energy. The id operates on the basis of the **pleasure principle** and seeks immediate gratification of its instinctual drives and needs in order to avoid tension. To reduce tension, the id relies primarily on reflex actions (e.g., blinking, sneezing) and primary process thinking, which involves forming a dream, hallucination, or other mental image of an object that would satisfy the id's needs.

b. The Ego: The **ego** develops at about 6 months of age in response to the id's inability to gratify all of its needs. The ego operates on the basis of the **reality principle**: It defers gratification of the id's instincts until an appropriate object is available in reality, and it employs **secondary process thinking**, which is characterized by realistic, rational thinking and planning. The primary task of the ego is to mediate the often conflicting demands of the id and reality and, once it has developed, the superego.

c. The Superego: The **superego** emerges when a child is between 4 and 5 years of age and represents an internalization of society's values and standards as conveyed to the child by his parents through their rewards and punishments. Behaviors that are rewarded by the child's parents become part of the child's ego ideal, while behaviors that are punished are incorporated into the **conscience**. In contrast to the ego, which postpones gratification of the id's instincts, the superego attempts to permanently block the id's socially unacceptable drives.

2. Developmental Theory: Freud's developmental theory proposes that the id's libido (sexual energy) centers on a different part of the body during each stage of development and that personality results from the ways in which conflicts at each stage are resolved. Failure to resolve a conflict at any stage often stems from excessive or insufficient gratification of the id's needs and can result in fixation at that stage.

Freud's **stages of psychosexual development** and the personality outcomes associated with fixation at a particular stage are summarized below.

Oral stage (birth-1 year): The mouth is the focus of sensation and stimulation during this stage, and weaning is the primary source of conflict. **Fixation** at the oral stage produces such personality traits as dependence, passivity, envy, manipulativeness, sarcasm, and orally focused habits (smoking, nail-biting, overeating, etc.). Other traits associated with the oral character include gullibility/suspiciousness, optimism/pessimism, and cockiness/self-belittlement. Some theorists suggest that orally fixated individuals waver from one pole of a dimension to the other (e.g., gullibility to suspiciousness, admiration to envy, or manipulativeness to passivity).

Anal stage (1-3 years): The main issue during this stage is control of bodily wastes, and conflicts stem from issues related to toilet training. **Fixation** produces anal retentiveness (stinginess, selfishness, obsessive-compulsive behavior) or anal expulsiveness (cruelty, destructiveness, messiness).

Phallic stage (3-6 years): Sexual energy is centered in the genitals during the phallic stage. The primary task is the resolution of the **Oedipal conflict**, which is marked by a desire for the opposite-sex parent and a view of the same-sex parent as a rival. A successful outcome results from identification with the same-sex parent and development of the superego. **Fixation** can produce a phallic character, which involves sexual exploitation of others.

Latency stage (6-12 years): Libidinal energy is diffuse rather than focused on any one area of the body. The emphasis is on developing social skills rather than achieving sexual gratification.

Genital stage (12+ years): Libido is again centered in the genitals. Successful outcome in this stage occurs when sexual desire is blended with affection to produce mature sexual relationships.

3. Anxiety: Anxiety is another essential component of Freud's personality theory. Freud described anxiety as an unpleasant feeling linked with excitement of the autonomic nervous system and proposed that its function is to alert the ego to impending internal or external threats (i.e., to danger arising from a conflict between the id's impulses and the demands of the superego or reality or from an actual threat in the external environment). When the ego is unable to ward off danger through rational, realistic means, it may resort to one of its defense mechanisms.

4. Defense Mechanisms: The various defense mechanisms all share two characteristics: (a) They operate on an unconscious level and (b) they serve to deny or distort reality. Common defense mechanisms include the following:

- **Repression** occurs when the id's drives and needs are excluded from conscious awareness by maintaining them in the unconscious. (Freud's **topographical model** of the mind divides it into three areas – the conscious, preconscious, and unconscious. Material in the preconscious is accessible to the conscious, but material in the unconscious is not.) Repression is considered the most "basic" defense mechanism because it is also the goal of all other defense mechanisms and the foundation of all neuroses.

- **Regression** occurs when a person retreats to an earlier, safer stage of development and behaves in ways characteristic of that stage.

- **Projection** involves attributing one's own unacceptable instinctual needs and drives to another person. Projection is derived from the primitive thought process of egocentrism.

- In **reaction formation**, the person avoids an anxiety-evoking instinct by actively expressing its opposite.

- **Displacement** involves the transfer of an instinctual drive from its original target to a less threatening target so that the drive can be more safely expressed.

- **Sublimation** is a type of displacement in which an unacceptable impulse is diverted into a socially acceptable, even admirable, activity. Sublimation is considered to be a "mature" defense mechanism (i.e., it is common in "healthy" adults).

- In **denial**, the individual admits that an anxiety-evoking impulse, thought, etc., exists, but denies that it is personally relevant. Denial is a relatively primitive defense mechanism and is related to a child's faith in the magical power of thoughts and words.

- The opposite of projection, **introjection** involves ascribing the thoughts and behaviors of others to oneself to better control one's affective responses to those thoughts and behaviors. Introjection is typically operative at a very early age.

- **Rationalization** occurs when an individual interprets his behaviors in a way that makes them seem more rational, logical, and/or socially acceptable. This defense rarely appears before adolescence.

- **Undoing** occurs when a person repeatedly engages in a behavior to undo the effects of a past action that he has found to be unacceptable. The behavior is typically the opposite of the unacceptable action.

- **Isolation of affect** involves severing the conscious psychological connection between an unacceptable impulse or behavior and its original memory source; the person remembers the experience but separates it from the affect associated with it.

5. Defense Mechanisms and Dysfunctional Behavior: While defense mechanisms can be considered adaptive because they serve to reduce anxiety, they can lead to dysfunctional behavior if they become the ego's habitual way of dealing with danger. Because reliance on a defense mechanism prevents the ego from actually resolving the conflict or other threat that caused the anxiety, anxiety can re-emerge under certain conditions (e.g., when a person experiences extreme stress) and produce undesirable symptoms. With regard to specific symptoms or dysfunction, some psychodynamic theorists have proposed the following with regard to the defense mechanisms: (a) Reaction formation, isolation of affect, and undoing have been associated with *obsessive-compulsive personalities*. (b) Displacement is thought to underlie obsessions. (c) Individuals with *paranoia* are believed to "project" their own threatening or unacceptable impulses onto others (projection). (d) Introjection and regression are thought to underlie *depression*. For example, the person internalizes the anger he feels toward someone else. (e) For people addicted to substances, ambivalence to change has been associated by some theorists with high levels of projection, denial, and rationalization. For instance, projection is used to rid oneself of uncomfortable feelings by attributing them to someone or something else, and a person with alcoholism might say, "I drink because nobody cares about me."

Object-Relations Personality Theories

The object-relations theorists consider object-seeking (relationships with others) as a basic inborn drive, and they emphasize a child's early relationships with objects, especially the child's internalized representations (**introjects**) of objects and **object relations**. The object-relations theorists include Melanie Klein, Ronald Fairbairn, Margaret Mahler, and Otto Kernberg. Each of these object-relations theorists has a unique theory of personality development.

1. Mahler's Phases of Identity Development: Mahler focuses on the processes by which an infant assumes his own physical and psychological identity.

Her **separation-individuation theory** proposes the following three phases:

Normal autism (first month of life): The infant is in a state of normal autism (detachment and self-absorption) and essentially oblivious to the external environment. If the infant's needs are fulfilled by his parents, he will move on to a normal state of symbiosis.

Normal symbiosis (age 2 to 3 months): The infant is aware of his mother, but has no sense of individuality (he doesn't differentiate between "I" and "not-I"); he and his mother are one (are "fused"). When the infant begins to recognize that others exist, he doesn't clearly discriminate them from the self. Over time, he comes to discriminate between pleasurable and painful qualities of experience involving others.

Separation-individuation (begins at about 4 months): The actual development of object relations occurs during the separation-individuation phase. "**Separation**" refers to the development of limits or the differentiation between the infant (self) and the mother; "**individuation**" refers to the development of the infant's ego, sense of identity, and cognitive abilities. The infant takes his first steps toward separation through sensory exploration of the environment and then, as his locomotor skills increase, by actual physical exploration. This is followed by a period of conflict between independence and dependence, which is manifested as **separation anxiety** (see "rapprochement," below). By about 3 years of age, the child has developed a permanent sense of self and object (**object constancy**) and is able to perceive others as both separate and related (Corey, 1991). For Mahler, this accomplishment is the foundation for mature relationships in which both positive and negative emotions can be expressed and the person can establish commitments to other people that don't threaten his own identity.

The separation-individuation phase is divided into three subphases, which often overlap in time: hatching (age 5 to 9 months), practicing (age 9 to 16 months), and rapprochement (age 15 months and beyond). During the **rapprochement** subphase, the child realizes that his emerging physical mobility demonstrates psychic separateness from his mother. He may become tentative, wanting his mother to be in sight so that he can safely explore his world. If the mother misreads this need and responds with impatience or unavailability, the child may develop an anxious fear of abandonment.

For object-relations theorists, maladaptive behavior is the result of abnormalities in early object relations. Mahler, in particular, traces adult psychopathology to problems that occurred during separation-individuation.

2. Splitting: Many of the object-relations theorists believe that, in infancy, there is a natural tendency to split mental representations of the self and others into "good" and "bad," and that inadequate resolution of this "splitting" is one of the causes of maladaptive behavior. For example, according to Kernberg, due to adverse childhood experiences, an individual with borderline personality disorder never integrated the positive and negative aspects of his experiences with others and, as a result, continues to shift back and forth between contradictory images (i.e., between overidealizing others and devaluating them).

Jung's Personality Theory (Analytical Psychotherapy)

Carl Jung adopted a broader view of personality development than Freud and defined libido as general psychic energy. He also believed that behavior is determined not only by past events, but also by future goals and aspirations.

From the perspective of Jung's analytical psychotherapy, personality is the consequence of both conscious and unconscious factors. The **conscious** is oriented toward the external world, governed by the ego, and represents the individual's thoughts, ideas, feelings, sensory perceptions, and memories. The **unconscious** is made up of the personal unconscious and collective unconscious. The personal unconscious contains experiences that were once conscious but are now repressed or forgotten or were unconsciously perceived; while the **collective unconscious** is the repository of latent memory traces that have been passed down from one generation to the next. Included in the collective unconscious are **archetypes**, which are "primordial images" that cause people to experience and understand certain phenomena in a universal way (Reisman, 1991). Archetypes of particular importance to personality development include the "self," which represents a striving for a unity of the different parts of the personality; the "persona," or public mask; the "shadow," or "dark side" of the personality; and the "anima" and "animus," which are, respectively, the feminine and masculine aspects of the personality. Jung also described the personality as consisting of two attitudes – extraversion and introversion – and four basic psychological functions – thinking, feeling, sensing, and intuiting. Although all four functions operate in the unconscious of all people, one function ordinarily predominates in consciousness.

In contrast to Freud, who emphasized the impact of the first six years of life on personality development, Jung viewed development as continuing throughout the lifespan and, in fact, was most interested in growth after the mid-30s. A key concept in Jung's personality theory is **individuation**, which refers to integration of the conscious and unconscious aspects of one's psyche, leading to the development of a unique identity. An important outcome of individuation is the development of wisdom, which occurs in the later years when one's interests turn toward spiritual and philosophical issues.

E. Erikson's Theory of Psychosocial Development

Although Erikson accepted Freud's emphasis on the role of unconscious motivation, he believed that Freud placed too much emphasis on the sexual basis for behavior. Erikson emphasized the role of other psychosocial motivations and needs that become the driving forces in development and behavior and placed greater emphasis on the ego than on the id – he assumed that people are basically rational and that behavior is due largely to ego functioning.

Erikson divided human development into eight stages that encompass the lifespan and proposed that a person has a **psychosocial task** to master during each stage: If the task is mastered, a positive quality becomes part of the personality and further development takes place; if the task is not mastered and the conflict is not resolved adequately, the ego is damaged because a negative quality is incorporated into it. Although no psychosocial crisis is ever completely resolved, a person must address the crisis of each stage sufficiently in order to meet the demands that arise during the next (and subsequent) stages of development.

The crises and positive outcomes associated with **Erikson's eight stages of psychosocial development** ("eight stages of man") are summarized below.

Basic trust vs. basic mistrust (infancy): A positive relationship with one's primary caregiver during infancy results in a sense of trust and optimism.

Autonomy vs. shame and doubt (toddlerhood): A sense of self (autonomy) develops out of positive interactions with one's parents or other caregivers.

Initiative vs. guilt (early childhood): Favorable relationships with family members result in the ability to set goals and devise and carry out plans without infringing on the rights of others.

Industry vs. inferiority (school age): The most important influences are people in the neighborhood and at school. To avoid feelings of inferiority, the school-age child must master certain social and academic skills.

Identity vs. role confusion (adolescence): Peers are the dominant social influence in adolescence. A positive outcome is reflected in a sense of personal identity and a direction for the future.

Intimacy vs. isolation (young adulthood): The main task is the establishment of intimate bonds of love and friendship. If such bonds are not achieved, self-absorption and isolation will result.

Generativity vs. stagnation (middle adulthood): The people one lives and works with are most important. A generative person exhibits a commitment to the well-being of future generations.

Ego Integrity vs. despair (maturation/old age): Social influence broadens to include all of humankind. The development of wisdom (an informed, detached concern with life in the face of death) and a sense of integrity require coming to terms with one's limitations and mortality.

F. Learning Theories

"Learning" has been defined as a relatively permanent change in potential performance or behavior as the result of experience. Some learning theorists believe that all learning is the result of connections between stimuli and responses (e.g., classical conditioning, operant conditioning). Others emphasize the internal cognitive processes in learning (e.g., observational learning).

Classical (Respondent) Conditioning

1. US, UR, CS, and CR: Ivan Pavlov investigated what became known as classical conditioning through a series of experiments with dogs in which he paired presentation of a neutral stimulus (e.g., a tone) that does not produce salivation with presentation of meat powder, which naturally elicits salivation. After several pairings, presentation of the neutral stimulus alone produced a salivation response. Pavlov concluded that learning occurs when a CS is repeatedly paired with a US that naturally elicits a UR, so that the CS itself eventually produces the CR:

- Pavlov called the stimulus that naturally elicits the target response (e.g., meat powder) the **unconditioned stimulus** (US or UCS) and its response (e.g., salivation in response to meat powder) the **unconditioned response** (UR or UCR).

- Pavlov called the neutral stimulus (e.g., a tone) the **conditioned stimulus** (CS), and the response it produced after conditioning (e.g., salivation in response to a tone) the **conditioned response** (CR).

2. Classical Extinction: Extinction refers to the elimination or weakening of a conditioned response. In classical conditioning, extinction occurs through repeated presentation of the CS without the US. The CS-CR relationship usually weakens, and the CR gradually disappears.

3. Stimulus Generalization and Stimulus Discrimination: Stimulus generalization is occurring when, after classical conditioning, a subject responds with a CR not only to the CS, but also to stimuli that are similar to it. Stimulus discrimination is the opposite of stimulus generalization: It refers to the ability to discriminate between similar stimuli and respond only to the CS with a CR, and it is established through selective reinforcement and extinction. Pavlov discovered "**experimental neurosis**" through his studies on stimulus discrimination: A dog being conditioned to make increasingly difficult discriminations between a circle and ellipses displayed restlessness, agitation, and unprovoked aggressiveness when the shape of an ellipse became too similar to that of a circle.

Operant Conditioning

B.F. Skinner considered Pavlov's model of classical conditioning adequate to explain the learning of respondent behaviors (behaviors, or reflexes automatically elicited by certain stimuli). He believed, however, that the majority of complex behaviors are operant behaviors that are voluntarily emitted as the result of the way they "operate" on the environment (i.e., as a result of the consequences that follow them). According to Skinner, the environment provides a variety of positive and negative consequences (reinforcements and punishments), and these consequences cause an organism to either display or withhold the behaviors that preceded them.

Skinner's principles of reinforcement and punishment can be viewed as extensions of Thorndike's **law of effect**. Thorndike believed that learning results from connections that develop between stimuli and responses (connectionism), and, according to the original version of his law of effect, any response that is followed by "a satisfying state of affairs" is likely to be repeated, while any response that results in an "annoying state of affairs" is less likely to be repeated.

1. Reinforcement and Punishment: Reinforcements and punishments can be either positive or negative. The terms "positive" and "negative" are not synonymous with "pleasant" and "unpleasant." Instead, positive refers to the application of a stimulus, and negative refers to the removal or withholding of a stimulus.

a. Reinforcement: By definition, **reinforcement** increases the behavior that it follows.

- In **positive reinforcement**, performance of a behavior increases as the result of the *application* of a stimulus (reinforcer) following the behavior. For example, a parent praises her child when he cleans his room, and as a result of this praise the child cleans his room more often.

- In **negative reinforcement**, performance of a behavior increases because it is followed by the *termination* (removal) of an unpleasant stimulus. For example, a parent stops nagging her child to clean his room after the child cleans his room; when the child realizes that the nagging stops when he cleans his room, he begins to clean his room more often.

b. Punishment: By definition, **punishment** decreases the behavior that it follows.

- In **positive punishment**, the *application* of a stimulus following a behavior decreases that behavior. For example, you are given a speeding ticket for driving too fast and this causes you to stop speeding.

- In **negative punishment**, the *removal* of a stimulus following a behavior decreases that behavior. For example, a parent takes away a child's allowance when he has a tantrum and this causes the child to stop having tantrums.

2. Operant Extinction: Operant extinction refers to withholding (discontinuing) reinforcement from a previously reinforced behavior in order to decrease or eliminate that behavior. The disappearance of a conditioned response is usually gradual and, at first, the response may be more forceful (i.e., there may be "**response bursts**").

3. Schedules of Reinforcement: The effectiveness of positive reinforcement is determined by the schedule on which it is delivered. The rate at which a behavior is acquired is fastest when the behavior is reinforced on a **continuous schedule** (i.e., when reinforcement is presented after each response). However, because satiation and rate of extinction are high when a continuous schedule is used, once an operant behavior has been acquired, the best way to maintain the behavior is to switch to an intermittent (partial) schedule. ("Satiation" is the condition of being satisfied or gratified with regard to a particular reinforcer.) Skinner distinguished between four **intermittent schedules**:

Fixed interval (FI): The person is reinforced after a fixed period of time regardless of the number of responses made (e.g., hourly or weekly wages). These schedules tend to produce low rates of responding because the number of responses is unrelated to the delivery of reinforcement.

Variable interval (VI): The interval of time between delivery of reinforcers varies in an unpredictable way (e.g., pop quizzes will be given during a semester, but the amount of time between quizzes varies). Subjects respond at a steady, but relatively low rate.

Fixed ratio (FR): A reinforcer is delivered each time the subject makes a specific number of responses (e.g., workers are paid following completion of a specific number of units). Because the relationship between responding and reinforcement is explicit, subjects quickly learn that the greater the number of responses, the greater the reward. These schedules produce a relatively high, steady rate of responding, usually with a pause right after delivery of the reinforcement.

Variable ratio (VR): Reinforcers are provided after a variable number of responses (e.g., gamblers playing slot machines). Because the relationship between responding and reinforcement is unpredictable, these schedules produce the highest rates of responding and responses that are the most resistant to extinction.

Observational Learning (a Cognitive Learning Theory)

Cognitive learning theories emphasize internal thought processes that occur during learning and reject the assumption that external reinforcement is a necessary condition for learning to occur. Examples of these theories include latent learning (Tolman), insight learning (Kohler), and observational learning (Bandura).

The observational (social) learning model proposes that a person can simply observe another person (a model) perform a behavior and subsequently display that behavior himself without external reinforcement.

1. Cognitive Processes in Observational Learning: Based on his research, Bandura concluded that observational learning entails a change in cognition involving four processes:

Attentional – to learn the modeled behavior, the learner must attend to and accurately perceive it.

Retention – to reproduce the modeled behavior, the learner must symbolically process it in memory through verbal coding or visual imagery. Retention is improved by cognitive rehearsal.

Production – the learner must be able to accurately reproduce and rehearse the modeled behavior. Production is improved through practice and feedback.

Motivational – the learner must be motivated to learn and perform the modeled behavior. Motivation is increased when the learner is reinforced, but the reinforcement can be either internal (self-reinforcement), vicarious, or external.

2. Factors Affecting the Effectiveness of Observational Learning: Observational learning is most effective when it is combined with guided participation (progressive performance by the learner with assistance from a model). Some research suggests that this is due to the sense of **self-efficacy** (personal mastery) provided by successful performance of the target responses (Bandura, 1977).

The effectiveness of observational learning is also affected by characteristics of the model. Learners are more likely to imitate a model when (a) the model has high status or has had past success, (b) the model is perceived to be similar to the learner, (c) the model's behavior is visible and relevant to the learner's needs and goals, and (d) the model has been reinforced for engaging in the behavior (vicarious reinforcement).

G. Cognitive Theories

Beck (Cognitive Therapy)

Aaron Beck (1967, 1984) focuses on the impact of cognitive schemas, automatic thoughts, and cognitive distortions on emotions and behavior:

Schemas: **Schemas** are underlying cognitive structures, or patterns of assumptions, thoughts, and beliefs that determine how individuals codify, categorize, and interpret their experiences. People develop schemas that, for example, influence how they make self-assessments and how they evaluate interpersonal events. Schemas develop early in life and are the product of biological, developmental, and environmental factors.

Schemas can be either functional or dysfunctional and either dormant or active. Depressogenic schemas and other dysfunctional schemas may be dormant until they are activated by internal or external stress (e.g., by conditions similar to those under which they originally developed).

Automatic thoughts and cognitive distortions: Dysfunctional schemas impair reality testing and the ability to think reasonably and are manifested in irrational **automatic thoughts** and are supported by **cognitive distortions** (errors in logic). Common cognitive distortions include the following:

Arbitrary inference – drawing conclusions without evidence.

Overgeneralization – drawing general conclusions on the basis of one event.

Selective abstraction – attending to detail while ignoring the total context.

Personalization – erroneously attributing external events to oneself.

Polarized thinking – thinking in a black-or-white fashion.

According to Beck, each psychological disorder is characterized by a different cognitive profile. Depression, for example, involves the **cognitive triad** of a negative view of oneself, the world, and the future: Depressed people have low self-esteem, blame themselves for their failures, and believe their problems will get worse. In contrast, the cognitive profile of anxiety reflects an excessive form of normal survival mechanisms, which entails unrealistic fears about physical and psychological threats. Anxious individuals overestimate the risk and consequences of perceived dangers.

Ellis (Rational Emotive Behavior Therapy, REBT)

Albert Ellis views behavior as a chain of events – A, B, and C – where:

- A is the **external event** to which the individual is exposed;
- B is the **belief** the individual has about A; and
- C is the **emotion or behavior** that results from B.

In other words, an emotional or behavioral response to an external event is due to beliefs about that event rather than to the event itself.

According to Ellis (1985), the primary cause of neurosis is the continual repetition of certain common **irrational beliefs**, such as the belief that it is necessary to be loved by everyone or the belief that one should be thoroughly competent, intelligent, and achieving in all respects.

H. Role Theory

Role theory refers to a set of concepts that define how the behaviors of individuals are influenced by the different social positions they hold and the expectations that accompany those positions.

1. Key Concepts: Core concepts associated with role theory include the following:

Social role: A **social role** is defined in terms of fulfilling an established and regulated position in society (e.g., child, parent, sibling, spouse, employee, organization member, neighbor, immigrant, patient, parolee).

Role expectations: The content of a given social role includes a set of **role expectations**, which consist of beliefs held by relevant others (family, cultural models, society, etc.) regarding how a person in that role should behave. A person's patterned behaviors often are influenced by his various social roles.

Role conception: **Role conception** refers to an individual's own beliefs and assumptions about how he is supposed to behave in a particular role. What an individual expects of himself may not conform to the role expectations defined by others and the wider society.

Role performance: **Role performance** (role enactment) refers to an individual's actual behavior while performing a role. A person's role performance may be consistent with his role conception, but not conform to others' role expectations.

Role demands: **Role demands** (role requirements) consist of the knowledge, skills, physical and mental abilities, and other personal attributes an individual must have in order to successfully perform a given role.

2. Sources of Social Role Problems: Broadly speaking, a social role problem involves either difficulties in fulfilling social role obligations or conflicts in relationships with family members and/or people at work or school or in the community. In some cases, a person may have a distorted view of his social role obligations (e.g., he may feel pressure or distress because he misunderstands how others expect him to behave). Social role problems can occur for any of the following reasons:

Role ambiguity (role confusion): A problem may emerge when there is a lack of clarity about the role expectations associated with a social role; this tends to occur in times of rapid social change. The individual is unsure of what is expected of him and unable to evaluate his own performance. Role ambiguity can result in insecurity and interpersonal conflict.

Role conflict: A problem may emerge when a person is faced with opposing role expectations within one social role (intra-role conflict) or with opposing expectations associated with two different social roles (inter-role conflict).

Self-role incongruence: A problem may emerge when there is little overlap between the requirements of a role and the individual's personality (e.g., a person finds that his values or lifestyle conflict with the expectations of a role).

Role overload: A problem may emerge when a person occupies more roles than he can perform adequately. Because most people cannot conform to the expectations of all their social roles, most people live with some degree of **role strain**. Role strain requires a person to make compromises and trade-offs, set priorities, and use defense mechanisms and coping strategies to reconcile his role conceptions with his limited time and energy.

Role loss: A problem may emerge when a person leaves a social role and, therefore, is no longer faced with familiar role expectations. Role loss can produce insecurity, depression, and/or confusion.

Role incapacity: A problem may emerge when an individual cannot adequately perform a social role. Possible reasons for this include physical or mental illness, a lack of needed knowledge or skills, drug addiction, intellectual disability, and so on. Some people don't learn how to perform expected role behaviors because of inadequate socialization (i.e., inadequate information or support or a lack of engagement in the socialization, or role induction, process). Other people have difficulty fulfilling their social role obligations because they lack sufficient resources from the environment.

Role rejection: A problem may emerge when a person refuses to perform a role (e.g., a parent abandons his child).

3. Types of Social Role Problems: Specific types of social role functioning problems are described on the following list (Karls & Wandrei, 1996). For some individuals, a social role problem will involve a mixture of these types.

Power: This can include the misuse or abuse of psychological or physical power and may result in serious interpersonal conflict, assault, and other forms of abuse.

Ambivalence: With ambivalence, a person has conflicting feelings about another individual or a life circumstance, often due to specific role performance expectations. For example, a person might be ambivalent about remaining in his marriage. This social role problem can result in a state of internal tension and lead to role performance behavior that upsets, annoys, angers, or confuses other people.

Responsibility: This relates to the obligation to comply with social role demands. Distress or unhappiness may emerge when a person finds his obligations overwhelming, suffocating, or difficult to perform (e.g., a father feels unable to meet the responsibilities of providing for his family). Self-esteem may suffer when a person recognizes that he hasn't fulfilled, or can't fulfill, his role obligations.

Dependency: A person's role performance may be dysfunctional because his dependency needs are not met. Dysfunctional role performance, rebellion, anger, or frustration may also occur when a person encounters or perceives obstacles to achieving normal independence. Over time, this can lead to depression and the loss of ambition and hope.

Loss: Loss may consist of the actual or threatened loss of a significant person by physical distance, the termination of a relationship, or death. This type of loss can interfere in a significant way with social role performance if it produces extreme anxiety, depression, hopelessness, anger, resentment, apathy, and/or lethargy.

In other cases, a person may experience the loss of a familiar or valued social role (i.e., a change in status or position) as the result of a life-cycle transition, life event, or physical impairment. Status changes usually require significant adjustment and lifestyle reorganization (i.e. when a person's customary social roles are disrupted, he has to adjust to new and possibly unwanted roles and, in some cases, this can result in distress and anxiety).

A problem involving loss may also occur when a person is uncertain about his status in a relationship or knows his status but is dissatisfied with it.

Isolation: Due to fear, shyness, or discomfort in a relationship or social role, a person may self-isolate in order to avoid the stress of active participation. This behavior can stem from past hurts or disappointments and, in some cases, becomes a chronic condition stemming from low self-esteem or a mental disorder. In other cases, a person in a new situation or new community may find it difficult to form new relationships or discover that his familiar social roles are no longer adaptive.

Victimization: A person may transform a fear of emotional or physical harm into a behavioral pattern in which he surrenders to his fear and gives up his power to deal with a victimizer in his life. Any person involved in a relationship in which he is, or feels, victimized or intimidated can suffer significant social-role functioning problems. Subsequent changes in other aspects of social functioning can then produce feelings of powerlessness and alienation. A person living with a persistent threat of harm, whether real or perceived, may also develop a sense of hopelessness and a chronic anticipation of future harm.

I. Social Psychology Research

Social psychologists "attempt to understand and explain how the thought, feeling, and behavior of individuals are influenced by the actual, imagined, or implied presence of others" (Allport, 1968, p. 3).

1. Interpersonal Relationships: The presence of a well-liked person can decrease physiological arousal and stress (Kissel, 1965). In addition, satisfactory affiliations are linked to a number of mental health and physical health benefits, including increased resistance to disease (e.g., Cohen et al., 1991).

a. Attraction: Attraction (liking) is affected by a number of factors, including those listed below:

- We tend to like competent and intelligent people more than their incompetent and unintelligent peers, and this is especially true when the competent person occasionally makes small blunders (Aronson & Linder, 1965).

- Although we generally like others who like us (and vice-versa), attraction to a person is actually maximized when the person's evaluation of us is initially negative but then becomes positive. This **gain-loss effect** is most likely to occur when the person's change in opinion is gradual and clearly reflects a true "change of heart" (Aronson & Linder, 1965).

- Attraction increases as perceived similarity in beliefs, attitudes, values, and personality increases. In terms of needs, some studies suggest that need similarity is most important for attraction, but others indicate that **need complementarity** is more critical, especially in long-term romantic relationships.

- As long as people don't initially dislike one another, their attraction to each other is likely to be increased by physical proximity (**propinquity**) and repeated exposure (Bornstein, 1992).

b. The Maintenance and Dissolution of Relationships: Several theories have been proposed to explain why people decide to remain in or leave relationships.

Social exchange theory: **Social exchange theory** predicts that the decision to remain in or leave a relationship depends on the costs and rewards of the relationship: We are likely to stay in a relationship when rewards exceed costs but leave when the costs are greater than the rewards. Some research suggests that social exchange theory is more predictive of relationships with strangers, acquaintances, and business associates than of relationships with family members and close friends because, in the latter relationships, we are much less likely to expect compensation for our contributions (e.g., Clark & Mills, 1993).

Equity theory: According to equity theory, our perceptions of equity (fairness) in a relationship are more important than the absolute magnitude of costs and rewards. We consider a relationship to be equitable and are likely to stay in it when we believe our reward/cost (input/outcome) ratio is proportional to the reward/cost ratio of the other person. In contrast, when we feel a relationship is inequitable, we experience distress and may decide to leave it. There are two types of inequity: We feel "underbenefitted" when our input/outcome ratio is less than the ratio of the other person and "overbenefitted" when our ratio is greater than the ratio of the other individual.

2. Social Influence and Personal Control:

a. Bases of Social Power: In order to exert influence over another person, a person must have some type of power. French and Raven (1959) and others identify six **bases of social power**:

Coercive – the influencing agent has control over punishments.

Reward – the influencing agent has control over valued rewards and resources.

Expert – the influencing agent is believed to have superior ability, skills, or knowledge.

Referent – the target is attracted to, likes, or identifies with the influencing agent.

Legitimate – the target believes that the influencing agent has legitimate authority.

Informational – the influencing agent possesses specific information that is needed by the target person.

b. Behavioral Effects of Social Influence: Kelman (1961) describes the various behavioral effects of social influence in the following way.

- **Compliance** (the most superficial response) occurs when the person changes his behavior in order to obtain a reward or avoid punishment. Compliance is public and doesn't involve a private change in opinions or attitudes. Reward and coercive power lead to compliance.

- **Identification** occurs when the person changes his behavior because he wants to be liked by or identified with another person. In this case, behavior change reflects a private change in opinion or attitude, but the change is maintained only as long as the person continues to like or admire the influencing agent. Referent power is likely to produce identification.

- **Internalization** occurs when the individual changes his behavior because he actually (privately) accepts the beliefs, attitudes, or behaviors of another person. Expert, legitimate, and informational power are most likely to result in internalization.

Additionally, Brehm's (1972) theory of **psychological reactance** predicts that, when an attempt at social influence causes a person to feel a loss of personal freedom, the person may respond by acting in a way that is the opposite of what is desired.

c. Individual Differences in the Perception of Personal Control:

Locus of control: According to Rotter (1966), people differ with regard to the amount of control they feel they have over their own lives; and a person's score on Rotter's Locus of Control Scale indicates the extent to which the person believes his behavior is controlled by fate, the political structure, and other external sources (**external locus of control**) or by free choice and free will (**internal locus of control**).

Research on locus of control suggests that "high internals" attribute their success to intrinsic factors and are more achievement-oriented, self-confident, and willing to work hard to achieve personal goals, are less anxious, suspicious, and dogmatic, and tend to be better adjusted than "high externals."

Self-efficacy beliefs: Self-efficacy is another characteristic that is closely tied to perceptions of personal control. Positive beliefs about one's self-efficacy include feeling competent, effective, and in control of one's life. A person's **self-efficacy beliefs** determine how much effort he is willing to exert and how long he will continue to act when faced with obstacles.

3. Self-Monitoring (Impression Management): According to Snyder (1987), people differ in terms of self-monitoring, or their need for and ability to manage the impression that others form of them. High self-monitors are most concerned about their "**public self**" and, consequently, strive to match their attitudes and behaviors to the situation. These individuals are very good at determining what behaviors, attitudes, and values are socially desirable or expected in a situation and at concealing their true feelings and opinions. In contrast, low self-monitors are guided primarily by their own beliefs and values and attempt to alter the situation to match their "**private self**."

4. Attitudes and Attitude Change: In working with people, mental health professionals often assume that they can predict behaviors from attitudes and that attitudes influence behavior; what follows from this is that, by changing a person's attitude, we may be able to change his behavior. There is not always a consistent relationship between attitudes and behavior, however, and this finding has led to the development of theories on attitudes known as consistency theories, including cognitive dissonance theory (see below). **Consistency theories** share the assumptions that cognitive consistency is a desirable state, that inconsistencies between cognitions cause unpleasant feelings, and that people are motivated to reduce such unpleasantness, often by altering one of their cognitions.

Festinger's (1957) **cognitive dissonance theory** predicts that, when people have two incompatible cognitions, they experience dissonance, which they attempt to relieve using one of several methods. For instance, in some situations, people change their attitudes or behaviors; in other situations, they add consonant information or downplay the importance of the inconsistency.

One of the findings of the research on cognitive dissonance theory is that, the more that people suffer for something, the more positively they evaluate it. For example, Aronson and Mills (1959) found that college women who underwent a severe initiation for what turned out to be a dull group said they liked the group more than women who underwent a mild initiation. Apparently, when women held two inconsistent cognitions ("I worked very hard to get into this group" and "This group is so dull that the initiation wasn't worth it"), they altered one of their cognitions to reduce dissonance (e.g., "This group is actually very interesting after all"). Another finding is that people often experience discomfort after choosing between two alternatives, and, to reduce their **post-decisional dissonance**, they change their evaluations of the two choices: they typically increase the value (attractiveness) of the chosen alternative and decrease the value of the unchosen alternative.

One of the best known studies on cognitive dissonance theory is Festinger and Carlsmith's (1959) investigation of **forced-compliance**, which involves requiring people to behave in ways that are counter to their private attitudes. Participants in their study first participated in a dull experiment and were then paid either $1.00 or $20.00 to tell potential participants that the experiment had been interesting and fun. When the original participants were later asked to evaluate the dull experiment, those who had been paid $20.00 accurately described it as boring, while those who had been paid $1.00 described it as enjoyable. Presumably, this was because, unlike the $20.00 participants, the $1.00 participants had insufficient justification for lying and, therefore, experienced dissonance, which they attempted to reduce by changing their attitude toward the experiment (i.e., by deciding that the experiment was enjoyable).

II. Human Development Over the Lifespan

A. Heredity and the Environment

1. The Role of Heredity: Heredity (genetic endowment) affects a person's development in several ways. Most traits are polygenic, which means that they are influenced by multiple genes. Height, weight, intelligence, and personality are polygenic traits. Other characteristics are the result of a single pair of genes that contains a dominant gene or two recessive genes. When a trait is due to a dominant gene, a child who is either homozygous (has inherited the gene from both parents) or heterozygous (has inherited the gene from only one parent) will exhibit that trait. When a trait is due to a recessive gene, a child must be homozygous with regard to that gene in order to display the trait.

The contribution of heredity to an observed characteristic is expressed in terms of a "heritability estimate," which indicates the extent to which "phenotype" varies within a group of people as the result of differences in "genotype." **Genotype** refers to a person's genetic inheritance, while **phenotype** refers to his observed characteristics, which are due to a combination of heredity and environment. As an example, a person whose parents are both very tall may have the genes for "tallness" but end up shorter than his genetic make-up dictates due to illness or poor diet.

2. The Nature-Nurture Debate: Human development is currently viewed by most developmental psychologists as being due to a combination of genetic and environmental factors, and the current "nature-nurture debate" focuses on the relative contributions of these factors and how they interact to produce behavior. For example, some experts propose that there is a genetically determined **range of reaction** for certain traits and that an individual's status within that range depends on environmental factors. Others point out that the relative importance of heredity and the environment differs at various points in the lifespan, with heredity being most critical during the early stages of development and environmental factors predominating during later stages. Because of the difference in the impact of nature and nurture over the lifespan, it is possible to make more accurate generalizations about 2 year olds than about 72 year olds: As people age, they become more diverse as their behaviors become less the consequence of genetically determined patterns and more the result of a wide range of environmental influences.

Some theorists believe that while both nature and nurture influence development, they are moderated by culture. **Cultural context theory** proposes that depending on the cultural context (i.e., the way an event is experienced and interpreted), the same factor will have different effects on development. Researchers associated with this view include Bronfenbrenner and Erikson.

3. Human Plasticity: The concept of human plasticity (capacity for change) suggests that variations in the environment can affect a person's cognitive functioning, social functioning, personality, physical health, and mental health, independent of his genetic endowment. An example is a person who is genetically predisposed to develop schizophrenia during his lifetime but never develops schizophrenia – this demonstrates that biological factors by themselves don't explain the development of schizophrenia. A related theory is the **diathesis-stress theory** (a.k.a. stress-diathesis theory), which proposes that schizophrenia and some other mental disorders are the result of genetic predisposition combined with stressful situations in the environment.

4. Critical Periods and Sensitive Periods: A **critical period** is a specific, predetermined period of time during biological maturation when an organism is particularly sensitive to certain stimuli that can have either a positive or negative impact on development. Critical periods were originally described by **ethologists** who found that an organism must be exposed to particular environmental stimuli during specific periods for a behavior to develop. For example, Lorenz (1965) found that the critical period for imprinting in geese occurs during the first two or three days after birth. Developmental psychologists have subsequently identified several critical periods for various aspects of physical development in humans, but there is less certainty about their existence for other aspects of behavior. Consequently, most experts agree that, for many human behaviors (e.g., attachment and language), there are sensitive periods rather than critical periods. **Sensitive periods** are longer in duration and more flexible than critical periods, and they are not tied as closely to chronological age or maturational stage.

B. Physical Growth and Development

Prenatal Development

1. Stages of Prenatal Development: Prenatal development occurs in three stages: (a) *Germinal stage:* The first two weeks make up the germinal stage, and, during this stage, the fertilized ovum is called a zygote. (b) *Embryonic stage:* The embryonic stage includes the beginning of the third week through the eighth week. The embryo secretes human chorionic gonadotropin (HCG), and HCG can be detected in the mother's blood six to eight days after conception. An at-home pregnancy test can detect HCG in the urine as soon as one day after a missed menstrual cycle. (c) *Fetal stage:* The fetal stage begins at the onset of the ninth week and continues until birth. After eight weeks, the embryo is 90 percent formed and looks like a human being. From this point on, it is referred to as a fetus. A fetus is full term and ready for life outside the uterine environment between 38 and 41 weeks.

2. Potential Pregnancy Complications:

a. Toxemia and Eclampsia: The early stages of **toxemia** (which are called preeclampsia) may not be detected until a prenatal visit because many women don't notice their symptoms. The symptoms of **preeclampsia** include elevated blood pressure, swelling (especially of the face and hands), weight gain, and protein in the urine. Untreated preeclampsia can progress to **eclampsia** (severe toxemia), which can lead to maternal death, fetal death, and fetal brain damage.

b. Intrauterine Growth Retardation: **Intrauterine growth retardation** (IUGR) has occurred when fetal weight is below the 10th percentile for gestational age. This condition is caused by factors that alter the environment in the uterus, resulting in intrauterine deprivation and slowed fetal growth. Examples of these factors include the mother's nutrition, health status, level of environmental stress, and use of cigarettes, alcohol, or other drugs. IUGR is associated with an increased risk of fetal death and problems for the infant following birth (see also "small-for-gestational age" infants in this section).

3. Causes of Birth Defects: Causes of birth defects include chromosomal disorders, exposure to teratogens, poor maternal health, and complications during the birth process (the latter are reviewed under The Birth Process, which follows this discussion).

a. Chromosomal Disorders: All human cells (except the sperm and ovum) contain 46 chromosomes that are arranged in 23 pairs. Twenty-two pairs of chromosomes are autosomes, while the 23rd pair contains the sex chromosomes. When a disorder is carried on an autosome, it is referred to as an autosomal disorder; when it is carried on a sex chromosome, it is referred to as sex-linked. Disorders related to the chromosomes are the result of the inheritance of a single dominant gene or two recessive genes or a chromosomal abnormality.

Disorders due to dominant genes: Dominant gene disorders are due to the inheritance of a single dominant gene from one parent. Huntington's disease is an example of an autosomal dominant gene disorder.

Disorders due to recessive genes: Recessive gene disorders are due to the inheritance of a pair of recessive genes (one from each parent). Examples of recessive gene disorders include cystic fibrosis, sickle cell disease, Tay-Sachs disease, and **phenylketonuria (PKU)**. PKU involves an inability to metabolize the amino acid phenylalanine, which is found in high-protein foods. If detected early with a blood test, its symptoms can be prevented by a diet low in phenylalanine. If untreated, PKU usually produces moderate to profound intellectual disability.

Disorders due to a chromosomal abnormality: Some of these disorders are the result of too many or too few chromosomes and others are due to alterations in chromosome structure (deletions, translocations, or inversions). **Down syndrome** is an autosomal disorder usually caused by the presence of an extra chromosome 21. It is characterized by intellectual disability, retarded physical growth and motor development, distinctive physical features, and increased susceptibility to Alzheimer's dementia, leukemia, and heart defects. There is some evidence that the risk for giving birth to a baby with Down syndrome increases as the mother's (and possibly the father's) age increases.

b. Teratogens: **Teratogens** are substances that cross the placental barrier and cause defects in the embryo or fetus. The different organs are most susceptible to the effects of teratogens at different times, but, overall, exposure during the embryonic stage is most likely to cause major structural abnormalities.

Alcohol: Fetal alcohol spectrum disorders (FASDs) are a group of conditions that can occur in a child whose mother drank alcohol during pregnancy. FASDs include the following: (a) **Fetal alcohol syndrome** (FAS) is the most severe FASD. The symptoms of FAS vary, depending on the amount of alcohol consumed, but may include abnormal facial features, retarded physical growth, heart defects, intellectual disability, hyperactivity, irritability, and central nervous system (CNS) problems. A person with FAS may have problems with learning, memory, attention span, communication, vision, or hearing. The risk for FAS is highest, and the symptoms are most severe, when the mother drinks heavily every day or, in the early stages of pregnancy, engages in binge drinking.

Most symptoms of FAS are irreversible and persist into adulthood. Prevention of FAS involves teaching pregnant women about nutrition and the harmful effects of drinking during pregnancy. (b) **Alcohol-related neurodevelopmental disorder** (ARND) is associated with learning and behavioral problems (e.g., difficulties with math, memory, attention, judgment, and poor impulse control). (c) **Alcohol-related birth defects** (ARBDs) may include heart, kidney, bone, and/or hearing problems. In the past, ARNDs and ARBDs were referred to as "fetal alcohol effects."

Nicotine: Cigarette smoking is associated with placental abnormalities that can cause fetal death and stillbirth. Babies born to mothers who smoke are at higher risk for a low birth-weight, sudden infant death syndrome (SIDS), and respiratory diseases, and may have emotional and social disturbances and cognitive deficits.

Lead: Exposure to lead during prenatal development may result in a low birth-weight and intellectual disability.

Heroin/methadone: Maternal use of heroin or methadone during pregnancy is associated with toxemia, IUGR, miscarriage, premature birth, low birth-weight, stillbirth, sudden infant death syndrome (SIDS), and neonatal addiction with withdrawal symptoms (restlessness, vomiting, tremors).

c. *Maternal Health During Pregnancy:* A variety of infections, diseases, and other conditions that affect a pregnant woman can affect her developing embryo and fetus.

TORCH complex: Several nonbacterial infections known collectively as the TORCH complex can cause complications such as miscarriage and fetal death and, if the baby survives, blindness, deafness, brain damage, and/or intellectual disability. These infections include toxoplasmosis (an infection caused by a parasite found in raw meat and cat feces); rubella (German measles); the viral infection cytomegalovirus; and active herpes. For instance, if a pregnant woman is infected with **rubella**, especially during the first trimester, her infant is at high risk for heart defects, blindness, deafness, and intellectual disability.

HIV/AIDS: The risk that an infected mother will transmit HIV to her infant is significantly reduced when the anti-HIV drug AZT is administered to the mother during pregnancy and delivery. Babies with HIV are frequently small for gestational age and most of them show signs of the virus during the first year of life (e.g., greater-than-normal susceptibility to infections, enlarged liver and spleen, swollen lymph nodes, and oral candidiasis). In early childhood, these children have immunologic abnormalities and delays in physical and cognitive development.

Syphilis: Syphilis can be passed to the fetus through the placenta, and fetal infection with syphilis can result in miscarriage or eye, ear, bone, or brain damage.

Maternal malnutrition: Maternal malnutrition during prenatal development is associated with miscarriage, stillbirth, low birth-weight, intellectual disability, and other problems. Severe malnutrition in the third trimester (especially protein deficiency) is particularly harmful to the developing brain. The Special Supplemental Nutrition Program for Women, Infants, and Children (WIC) is designed to help ensure adequate nutrition for low-income women during pregnancy. For some pregnant women, malnutrition is caused when **pica** interferes with their appetite for normal food. Pica involves the ingestion of nonfood substances (paint chips, dirt, ice, etc.) and is sometimes a cultural phenomenon.

Stress: If a woman experiences severe or prolonged emotional stress during pregnancy, she is at higher risk for miscarriage, painful labor, and premature delivery, and her baby is more likely to have a low birth-weight, be hyperactive and irritable, and exhibit irregular feeding, sleeping, and bowel habits. The effects of stress may be reduced when the woman has adequate social support during her pregnancy.

d. Spousal/Partner Abuse: Spousal/partner battering often begins or grows worse while a woman is pregnant and increases the risk of miscarriage, preterm labor, and low birth-weight. Moreover, because of the stress they are under, battered women are more likely to have poor health habits and may abuse substances. Many battered women are socially isolated and some lack access to prenatal care.

4. Promoting Healthy Fetal Development: Ways of promoting optimal fetal development include encouraging early and ongoing prenatal care and good health practices, identifying and treating substance abuse, providing parent education, and facilitating adequate social support. Women in poor communities may face barriers to accessing prenatal care, however, and, even when health care is available, a woman may have cultural beliefs about health care practices that don't emphasize the need for early and regular prenatal care (Ashford et al., 2006). Additionally, women who are chronic or heavy alcohol or other drug users usually receive inadequate prenatal care and have poor prenatal nutrition. Some of these women need to be referred to support groups or classes to help ensure healthy pregnancy outcomes.

5. Drug Testing of Pregnant Women: Laws allowing a pregnant woman to be tested and treated for substance abuse without her consent and be jailed if she does not comply with treatment have raised ethical issues for health care providers. Moreover, studies show that when such laws were enforced, a woman's race, ethnicity, and socioeconomic status had a major impact on whether or not she was tested without her consent (Mitchell, 1993). Following a Supreme Court decision in 2001 (Ferguson vs. City of Charleston), the current practice is to avoid criminalizing drug use among pregnant women and to ensure that doctors and social service agencies offer treatment before maternal drug use has had a chance to harm the developing fetus.

The Birth Process

1. Potential Birth Complications:

a. Anoxia: Prolonged anoxia (oxygen shortage) during the birth process can be caused by several factors including a twisted umbilical cord or the narcotics given to the mother during the birth process. Potential consequences of anoxia include delayed motor and cognitive development, intellectual disability, and, in severe cases, cerebral palsy.

b. Herpes Simplex 2: Infants exposed to herpes simplex 2 during the birth process are at high risk for death, brain damage, and blindness. It is common to deliver babies through cesarean section when the mother is infected with the herpes virus.

c. Gonorrhea: If a woman with gonorrhea passes the infection to her baby during birth, the baby may become blind. Most hospitals treat a newborn's eyes with erythromycin ointment or silver nitrate to prevent this complication.

2. Premature Infants: An infant born prior to 37 weeks is considered premature. The risk for prematurity has been linked to a number of factors including low socioeconomic status (SES), teen motherhood, maternal malnutrition, and maternal drug use.

a. Potential Complications: (a) A baby born before the lungs are fully mature can suffer from **respiratory distress syndrome** (RDS) and need a ventilator to assist with breathing. (b) Premature infants may experience **apnea** (periods when they stop breathing), most commonly after exertion, such as following a feeding. (c) Because the sucking reflex is not well developed until 34 weeks of gestation, some premature babies are unable to nurse or drink from a bottle and must be fed through a tube (gavage feeding) until they learn to suck. (d) Finally, preterm infants are at higher-than-normal risk for **jaundice** (hyperbilirubinemia), a condition caused by a buildup of bilirubin and resulting in a yellowish-orange color to the skin. High levels of bilirubin in the brain can lead to brain damage and possible intellectual disability. Babies with jaundice are usually placed under lights that help to break down the bilirubin.

b. Outcomes for Premature Infants: The majority of premature infants now survive, especially those with a birth-weight of at least 1500 grams (3.3 pounds). In the absence of significant abnormalities and with appropriate medical attention and a supportive environment, premature infants often catch up to their nonpremature peers in terms of cognitive, language, and social skills by 2 or 3 years of age (Greenberg & Crnic, 1988).

In addition, studies have confirmed the importance of touch for newborn premature infants (e.g., Harrison et al., 1991). Parental touch, for example, is associated with better weight gain, improved development of the nervous system, and more rapid development.

3. Small-for-Gestational Age Infants: When a newborn's weight is below the 10th percentile for his gestational age, the infant is small-for-gestational age (SGA). Regardless of gestational age at birth, SGA infants have developed at a less-than-normal rate and, as a result, are at high risk for asphyxia during birth, respiratory disease, hypoglycemia, and other problems.

The Physical Development of Newborns

1. Newborn Evaluations: A commonly used measure of newborn health is the **Apgar score**, which is obtained using a scale that examines the newborn's adaptation to life outside the womb. At 1 minute and 5 minutes after birth, the physician evaluates the baby's skin coloration, heart rate, response to stimulation, muscle tone, and breathing effort, and, in each of these five areas, gives him a score of 0, 1, or 2. Babies who score from 5 to 7 ("poor") may need medical intervention, and babies who score 0 to 4 ("very poor") usually require resuscitation. A very poor score at 5 minutes is associated an increased risk of neurological problems.

2. Newborn Reflexes: Reflexes are unlearned responses to particular stimuli in the environment. Newborn reflexes include the following:

Babinski – toes fan out and upward when soles of the feet are tickled.

Rooting – turns head in the direction of touch applied to the cheek.

Moro (startle) – flings arms and legs outward and then toward the body in response to a loud noise or sudden loss of physical support.

Stepping (walking) – makes coordinated walking movement when held upright with feet touching flat surface.

The **Brazelton Neonatal Assessment Scale** (**BNAS**) can be used with infants up to age 1 month to assess their reflexes, muscle tone, response to stimulation, and other characteristics. The scale is helpful for evaluating how infants use different responses and states of consciousness to control their reactions to environmental stimulation (e.g., an overstimulated baby may cry, look away, or fall asleep).

3. The Newborn's Bones: At birth, an infant's bones are soft and pliable. During infancy, the bones harden to allow the child to stand and walk. **Fontanelles** (soft spots) are locations in a normal infant's skull where several of the bones do not join together. By age 2, these spots fill in and harden. Doctors often examine the fontanelles when assessing the hydration of infants.

Physical Development in Infancy and Toddlerhood

1. Brain Development in Infancy (Through Adolescence): Whereas the lower centers of the brain are sufficiently developed at birth to control life-maintaining reflexes, the **cerebral cortex** (the part of the brain responsible for higher-level cognitive functions, language, spatial skills, and complex motor activities) is almost completely undeveloped. During the first few months of life, the primary motor and sensory areas of the cortex undergo substantial development, and the frontal cortex continues to mature through adolescence. This means that higher-level cognitive functions continue to develop in adolescence, and an older adolescent may be more capable than a younger one of making good decisions and judgments.

2. Early Physical Milestones: The ages at which early milestones are reached vary from child to child, and the experts often report somewhat different ages. Generally, however, a baby may need **developmental assessment** if he fails to demonstrate a skill at an age when 90 percent of babies can perform that skill. Note, too, that while age norms for motor development vary culturally, infants the world over obtain motor milestones in the same sequence. Milestones in physical development during the first four years of life are summarized below.

1-3 Months: Able to raise chin from ground and turn head from side-to-side. By the third month, can play with hands and fingers and brings objects in hand to mouth.

4-6 Months: By 4 months, rolls from abdomen to back. At 5 months, sits on lap and reaches and grasps. At 6 months, sits alone and stands with help. First teeth appear at 5 to 9 months.

7-9 Months: At 8 to 9 months, sits alone without support and begins crawling and creeping. At 9 to 10 months, pulls self to standing by holding furniture.

10-12 Months: At 10 to 11 months, stands alone and walks with help. At about 12 months, **takes first steps alone**.

13-15 Months: By 13 to 14 months, **walks alone** with a wide-based gait (about 50 percent walk alone well by 12 months and about 90 percent do so by 14 months). By 15 months, creeps up stairs, scribbles spontaneously, and uses a cup well.

16-24 Months: By 18 months, runs clumsily, walks up stairs with hand held, and can use a spoon. By 24 months, goes up and down stairs alone, kicks ball, turns pages of a book, and 50 percent of children **use the toilet during the day**.

25-48 Months: At 30 months, jumps with both feet. By 36 months, rides a tricycle, dresses and undresses with simple clothing, and is usually **completely toilet trained**. By 48 months, exhibits a stable preference for the right or left hand.

3. Illness in Infancy: Babies are born with natural immunity to rubella, measles, mumps, polio, and diphtheria, but this immunity does not last past age 3 to 6 months. Therefore, **immunization** of infants is important and may need to be discussed with clients who are new parents.

- **Pertussis** (whooping cough) is still a significant problem in the U.S., despite the availability of a pertussis vaccine. This problem is most serious for infants and young children, who are at higher risk of disease complications.

- **Colic** involves daily episodes of intense, inconsolable crying that begin suddenly, may last from a few minutes to several hours, and then spontaneously resolve. Colic can develop between 2 and 6 weeks of age and has been attributed to food allergies, an immature digestive system, an immature nervous system, and an anxious caregiver. Colic affects about 25 percent of babies. Many babies outgrow colic by about 3 months of age, and 90 percent of all cases of colic resolve by age 9 months.

4. Sudden Infant Death Syndrome: Sudden infant death syndrome (SIDS) refers to the unexpected death of an infant for which no physical cause can be found and is the most common cause of death in the first year of life. The cause of SIDS is unknown, but certain infant risk factors have been identified: SIDS occurs more often in low-birth-weight infants, premature infants, infants with low Apgar scores, infants who sleep on their stomachs, infants with a sibling who previously died of SIDS, and male infants (Martinez, 1996). Maternal risk factors include young age, low socioeconomic status, smoking, drug abuse during pregnancy, closely spaced pregnancies, and inadequate prenatal care (Martinez, 1996). Parents who lose an infant to SIDS usually blame themselves for their child's death and need significant support.

5. Failure to Thrive: Failure to thrive occurs when a baby's weight falls below the 5th percentile for his age. Many failure-to-thrive babies are born at a normal weight but then markedly decrease their rate of weight gain. Nutritional deficits during infancy can have long-term effects, including growth deficits, developmental delays, intellectual disability, learning disorders, poor academic performance, and reduced resistance to infection.

Failure to thrive may be organic or nonorganic. In organic failure to thrive, there is an underlying medical condition that causes the slowed rate of growth. In **nonorganic failure to thrive**, no medical cause can be found. Risk factors associated with nonorganic failure to thrive include the following:

Maternal deprivation: Many mothers of failure-to-thrive infants were deprived in their own childhood, which may interfere with their ability to adequately meet their baby's emotional, feeding, and other needs. In turn, emotional deprivation of the infant may reduce the amount of growth hormone he produces, and emotional stress may increase the likelihood of appetite loss, vomiting, and diarrhea (Schuster & Ashburn, 1992).

Child factors: Failure to thrive also occurs when parents *do* meet their babies' emotional and other needs. Some babies are born with a temperament that makes them difficult to feed, babies with cerebral palsy and those born with low birth-weight or prematurely can be difficult to feed, and babies with chronic ear infections or other illnesses may feel too sick to eat.

Family factors: Family factors that have been associated with failure to thrive include high levels of stress; a chaotic lifestyle; depression, substance abuse, or domestic violence in the household; parents who are overly controlling and get into "food battles" with their baby; weight-conscious parents who minimize their baby's fat intake; parents who don't understand a baby's nutritional needs; and poverty. Poverty can make it difficult to purchase adequate or nutritious food, even with assistance from WIC or Temporary Assistance for Needy Families (TANF).

Physical Development in Childhood and Adolescence

1. Sleep: Because one of its main side-effects is sedation, Benadryl (diphenhydramine hydrochloride) is sometimes used by parents as a pediatric sleep aid to help their children fall and stay asleep at night. Research has found, however, that Benadryl can have a paradoxical effect in about 10 to 15 percent of children: It produces symptoms of hyperactivity in these children that keep them wake. Note that Benadryl should not be used often as a pediatric sleep aid or for a prolonged period of time, and, if a child is having difficulty sleeping, the parents should be advised to discuss possible reasons with the child's doctor.

Sleep experts maintain that adolescents need just over nine hours of sleep every night to maintain good physical and mental health. Consequences of insufficient sleep for adolescents include irritability, anxiety, depression, and impaired cognitive functioning (Dahl & Lewin, 2002).

2. Lead Poisoning: Lead is present in the environment from not only lead-based paint in older buildings but also from other sources, so that many children are at risk of lead poisoning. Because even low lead levels can affect cognitive abilities, experts recommend that all children with learning or behavior problems be screened for lead exposure (screening can be done using inexpensive blood testing). Early identification and treatment of lead exposure (e.g., removal of the child from the source of exposure, medications, use of air-filtration systems) can help prevent permanent damage.

3. Chronic Illness in Children and Adolescents: Approximately 30 percent of children have chronic health problems, with the most common problems being respiratory allergies, recurrent ear infections, and asthma (Newacheck & Taylor, 1992). **Bilateral otitis media with effusion** (inflammation of the left and the right middle ear, with fluid leakage) is a severe form of middle ear infection. Middle ear infections in early childhood, especially severe infections resulting in hearing loss, have been associated with the development of learning disorders later in childhood.

a. Adjustment to Chronic Illness: Children and adolescents with chronic medical conditions are at higher risk for both internalizing symptoms (e.g., depressed mood) and externalizing symptoms (e.g., acting out), although most do not meet the criteria for a formal DSM diagnosis (Harbeck-Weber & Peterson, 1996). They also have higher-than-normal rates of school-related problems. School difficulties can be the direct result of the illness itself, may be caused by the medical treatment, or may be due to the child's frequent absences from school.

Hospitalized children are at risk for emotional and behavioral problems, and a major contributor to this risk is the child's separation from his family. Recognition of the impact of separation has resulted in increased visitation hours at hospitals and "rooming-in" (allowing parents to stay with their hospitalized children).

b. Factors Correlating With Better Adjustment: Illness severity is one of the best predictors of outcome for chronically ill children and adolescents, with less serious illness (especially low functional impairment) being associated with better overall adjustment (Garrison & McQuiston, 1989). Other factors predictive of good adjustment include higher socioeconomic status, a two-parent family, little visible disfiguration, and healthy parental adjustment.

c. Disclosure: There is evidence that children with cancer, HIV infection, and other life-threatening illnesses have better psychological outcomes when they are given accurate and developmentally appropriate information about their illness in its early stages (e.g., Gerson et al., 2001; Slavin, 1982). Therefore, in most situations, open communication with the child about his illness is advisable.

4. Obesity: Because eating habits established early in life often continue in adulthood, obese youngsters have a high risk of becoming obese adults. Obesity increases a person's risk of high blood pressure and certain diseases, including **diabetes**. It is also associated with psychological and social problems, including rejection or harassment by peers.

Physical Development and Change in Adulthood

1. Brain Development in Adulthood: By about age 30, the brain starts to gradually shrink as the result of a loss of neurons, and there is an acceleration of this brain atrophy after age 60. Other changes in the aging brain include the development of senile plaques, reduced blood flow to the brain, and a decrease in the level of some neurotransmitters. It appears, however, that the brain attempts to compensate for neuronal loss by developing new connections between the remaining neurons (Buell & Coleman, 1979). Also, there is recent evidence that new brain cells (neurons) develop during the adult years (Baringa, 1998).

2. Physical Changes in Late Adulthood: Increasing age is accompanied by a number of changes in sensory and psychomotor functioning, although the degree of change varies from person to person.

a. Vision: Most adults begin to notice some inability to focus on close objects (presbyopia) around age 40; and, after age 65, most experience visual changes that interfere with reading, driving, and other aspects of daily life. These age-related changes include loss of visual acuity, reduced perception of depth and color, increased light sensitivity, and deficits in visual search, dynamic vision (perceiving the details of moving objects), and speed of visual processing.

b. Audition: Many adults experience problems with hearing by age 40. However, the majority do not have significant hearing loss until after age 75; among individuals between the ages 75 and 79, at least 50 percent have hearing deficits that interfere with daily functioning. The biggest problem is a decreasing ability to perceive high-frequency sounds, which tends to occur earlier in men than in women and makes it difficult to understand human speech, especially when there is competing noise.

c. Strength, Coordination, and Reaction Time: Aging is associated with declines in strength and endurance, less efficient sensorimotor control, and increased reaction time. With regard to the latter, one of the most consistent findings is that normal aging is accompanied by behavioral slowing.

3. Physical Health in Late Adulthood: Although there is significant variation among individuals in the physical changes that occur with age, there is a predictable pattern of some physical decline, called "senescence," that naturally takes place as people age.

a. Physical Activity and Health: The benefits of regular physical activity in late adulthood include a lowered risk of coronary heart disease, colon cancer, diabetes, high blood pressure, and osteoporosis; reduced risk of falling; less anxiety and depression; greater ability to maintain joint strength and mobility; and better cognitive functioning. Maintaining lean muscle helps prevent frailty and disability.

b. Nutrition and Health: Older people may have difficulty meeting their nutritional needs for a variety of different reasons, including a reduced ability to smell and taste and changes in the body's ability to metabolize nutrients and water. The latter also increases vulnerability to dehydration. Additionally, low-income elders, those who are functionally impaired, and the very old who live alone may face financial and/or mobility problems that make it difficult to buy and prepare the foods required for a healthy diet.

c. Chronic Health Conditions: Most older adults with chronic health conditions do not experience significantly impaired functioning. The most common chronic health conditions among people over age 65 are hypertension and arthritis, followed by heart disease, sinusitis, and diabetes (Administration on Aging, 2003). **Osteoarthritis**, a degenerative joint disease, is the most common cause of disability among Americans over age 65, affecting men and women equally. Anti-inflammatory medication, a moderate exercise program, and the use of assistive devices can help an older person with arthritis retain his ability to function independently. Avoiding physical activity is not recommended because doing so causes the joints to become more stiff and painful over time.

Specific Factors Affecting Physical Health

1. Stress: Selye (1956) investigated physiological reactions to stress and concluded that people respond to all types of stressful situations in the same manner. This response, which Selye named the **general adaptation syndrome** (GAS), involves three stages:

Alarm reaction: In response to stress, the body releases higher levels of epinephrine (adrenaline). As a result, the body's glucose level rises and heart and respiration rates accelerate, thereby increasing the body's energy level.

Resistance: If the stress persists, breathing and heart rate return to normal levels, but the body signals the pituitary gland to release adrenocorticotropic hormone (ACTH). ACTH then activates the adrenal cortex to release the stress hormone **cortisol**, which maintains high blood glucose levels and increases the metabolism of fats and proteins.

Exhaustion: With prolonged stress, the pituitary gland and adrenal cortex lose their ability to maintain elevated hormone levels, and physiological processes begin to break down. Fatigue, depression, illness, or, in extreme cases, death, may occur.

As suggested by the GAS, the impact of prolonged stress on health is attributable, at least in part, to chronically elevated levels of cortisol and other stress hormones, which compromise the immune system (cause **immunosuppression**) by decreasing the production of lymphocytes (especially T cells) and antibodies, the body's major defenses against viruses, bacteria, and other antigens.

2. Socioeconomic Status: Socioeconomic status (SES) has a significant effect on health (Ashford et al., 2006). Alcohol and drug use, smoking, and unprotected sex are all more common among those with lower income and education. Additionally, people with lower income and education tend to experience higher levels of stress and more chronic stress, which increases vulnerability to illness and disease. Last, people living in poor communities may have less access to health care, and people with lower SES often lack health insurance (they can't afford to pay premiums, their jobs don't offer health benefits, etc.).

3. Gender: Women are more likely than men to seek and use health care and are more effective in using coping mechanisms and social support before, during, and after an illness. Men often do not prioritize their health or health care unless they are very ill and are more likely to use alcohol, drugs, and tobacco in response to stress (Ashford et al., 2006). In addition, males are more vulnerable than females to disorders that have been linked to biological factors, including certain physical illnesses (e.g., heart disease, cancer, and diabetes), intellectual disability, learning disabilities, and certain behavioral disorders (e.g., Halpern, 1997).

4. Culture/Race: Access to and quality of health care is generally better for whites than for non-whites. Key reasons for this appear to include language and cultural barriers; higher rates of poverty among nonwhites; and provider and institutional factors that include cultural and racial biases, ineffective communication, and insufficient outreach to minority communities.

Human Nervous System and Neurotransmitters

1. Divisions of the Human Nervous System: The *central nervous system* (CNS) consists of the brain and the spinal cord. The brain includes many substructures that are highly interrelated in terms of function. The *peripheral nervous system* (PNS) is made up of nerves that relay messages between the CNS and the body's sensory organs, muscles, and glands. The PNS is divided into the somatic nervous system and the autonomic nervous system: (a) The *somatic nervous system* (SNS) governs activities that are ordinarily considered voluntary. (b) The *autonomic nervous system* (ANS) is associated primarily with involuntary activities. Biofeedback, hypnosis, and other techniques have shown that some autonomic activities can be brought under voluntary control, however.

The ANS is further divided into the sympathetic and parasympathetic branches: (a) The *sympathetic branch* of the ANS is associated with arousal and the expenditure of energy and tends to act as a unit. In reaction to an external threat, for instance, the sympathetic branch causes dilation of the pupils, inhibition of peristalsis (muscle contractions in the digestive tract and elsewhere), dry mouth, sweating, and increased blood pressure and heart rate in order to ready the body for "**fight or flight**." (b) The *parasympathetic branch* of the ANS is involved in the conservation of energy and is active during digestion and periods of rest and relaxation. Biofeedback and other techniques used to foster the relaxation response do so by activating the parasympathetic branch. The parasympathetic branch is more specific in its actions than the sympathetic branch. For example, a cinder in the eye causes only tearing, not tearing, slowed heart rate, and lowered blood pressure.

2. Neurons: The neuron (nerve cell) is a specialized cell that is directly involved in mental processes and behavior. Most neurons consist of dendrites, the cell body (soma), and an axon. The job of the axon is to transmit information to other cells. Axons are often covered by a myelin sheath, which is a fatty substance that acts as an insulator and speeds up the conduction of nerve impulses.

3. Neurotransmitters: The relay of a nerve impulse between cells is usually chemically mediated and involves the release of a neurotransmitter into the small gap between neurons (the synapse). When released, neurotransmitters allow neurons to communicate with and affect each other. Some neurotransmitters excite neurons into action while others inhibit them. Some of the neurotransmitters that have been identified so far are described below.

Acetylcholine: Acetylcholine (ACh) causes muscles to contract and is involved in memory. Alzheimer's disease is associated with deterioration of ACh-secreting neurons in the brain.

Catecholamines: The catecholamines, including norepinephrine (noradrenaline), epinephrine (adrenaline), and **dopamine**, are involved in a number of functions including personality, mood, memory, and sleep: (a) Low levels of norepinephrine and dopamine are associated with some forms of depression. (b) Excessive activity at dopamine synapses has been linked to schizophrenia and Tourette's syndrome. (c) Dopamine is also involved in the regulation of movement, and degeneration of dopamine receptors underlies the muscular rigidity and tremors found in Parkinson's disease. (d) Elevated levels of dopamine in the brain have been implicated in the reinforcing actions of stimulant drugs, opiates, alcohol, and nicotine.

Serotonin (5-HT): **Serotonin** usually exerts an inhibitory effect and has been implicated in mood, hunger, temperature regulation, sexual activity, arousal, sleep, aggression, and migraine headache: (a) Elevated levels of serotonin contribute to schizophrenia and autism. (b) Low levels of serotonin play a role in depression, suicide, PTSD, obsessive-compulsive disorder, and aggression.

Gamma-aminobutyric acid (GABA): GABA, an inhibitory neurotransmitter, has been linked to sleep, eating, seizure, and anxiety disorders. GABA levels are affected by benzodiazepines and other CNS depressants, which are commonly used to treat anxiety. Degeneration of cells that secrete GABA contributes to the motor symptoms of Huntington's disease.

Glutamate: Glutamate plays a role in learning and memory and, more specifically, in long-term potentiation, a brain mechanism that is believed to be responsible for the formation of long-term memories. Excessive glutamate receptor activity can lead to seizures and may contribute to Huntington's disease, Alzheimer's disease, and other neurodegenerative disorders.

Endorphins: The endorphins have analgesic (pain-killing) properties and may be responsible for the pain relief produced by acupuncture. They have also been implicated in certain pleasurable experiences (e.g., the "runner's high") and the control of emotions, memory and learning, and sexual behavior.

C. Cognitive Growth and Development

Theories of Cognitive Development

1. Piaget's Constructivism: Piaget's theory of cognitive development is based on the premise that people actively construct higher levels of knowledge from elements contributed by both biological maturation and the environment.

For Piaget, the motivation for cognitive development arises from a drive toward cognitive equilibrium (**equilibration**). Development occurs when a state of disequilibrium brought on by a discrepancy between a person's current understanding of the world (repertoire of schemas) and reality is resolved through **adaptation**, which entails two complementary processes – "assimilation" and "accommodation." **Assimilation** is the incorporation of new knowledge into existing cognitive schemas (structures), while **accommodation** is the modification of existing schemas to incorporate new knowledge. When given a toy for the first time, a young child will treat it as he would any new object and will probably bang it, throw it, and taste it. In other words, the child will attempt to understand the toy by assimilating it into his current repertoire of schemas. As the child begins to recognize the toy's unique properties, he will adjust his existing schemas and, as a result, develop new ways of interacting with the toy; the latter process is referred to as accommodation.

Piaget described **four stages of cognitive development**, which he considered to be invariant and universal:

Sensorimotor stage (birth to 2 years): During this stage, thought is based on action: A child learns about objects through the sensory information provided by them (how they look, feel, and taste) and the actions that can be performed on them (sucking, grasping, hitting, etc.). An important accomplishment of the sensorimotor stage is the development of **object permanence** (the "object concept"), which emerges at about 8 months and allows the child to recognize that objects and people continue to exist when they are out of sight. Other important accomplishments are the beginning of an understanding of causality (recognition that certain events cause other events) and the emergence of deferred imitation and make-believe play. The former develops at about 10 months of age, and the latter at about 18 months.

Preoperational stage (2 to 7 years): A key characteristic of this stage is the symbolic (semiotic) function, which is an extension of symbolic thought and permits the child to learn through the use of language, mental images, and other symbols which stand for things that are not present. As a result of this capacity, preoperational children are able to engage in symbolic play and can solve problems mentally.

Despite the emergence of these abilities, the preoperational stage is limited by several factors, including the following: (a) Children in this stage exhibit precausal (transductive) reasoning, which reflects an incomplete understanding of cause and effect. One manifestation of precausal reasoning is **magical thinking**, or the belief that thinking about something will actually cause it to occur (e.g., thinking bad thoughts about Dad will cause something bad to happen to him). Another manifestation is **animism**, which is the tendency to attribute human characteristics to inanimate objects. A child is exhibiting animism when he says his stuffed bear gets lonely if it's not played with often enough. (b) Because of **egocentrism** (an inability to separate his own perspective from that of others), the preoperational child is unable to imagine another person's point of view. (c) Children in the preoperational stage do not recognize that actions can be reversed (**irreversibility**) and they focus on the most noticeable features of objects (**centration**). Consequently, these children are unable to conserve, or understand that changing one dimension of an object does not change its other dimensions. When a preoperational child watches a liquid being poured from a short fat glass into a tall thin one, for example, he is likely to say there is more liquid in the second glass.

Concrete operational stage (7 to 11 years): Children in this stage are capable of mental operations, which are logical rules for transforming and manipulating information. As a result, they are able to classify in more sophisticated ways (e.g., solve class inclusion problems), seriate, understand part-whole relationships in relational terms (e.g., bigger), and conserve. **Conservation** depends on the operations of **reversibility** and **decentration** and develops gradually, with conservation of number occurring first, followed by conservation of liquid, length, weight, and then displacement volume. Piaget used the term horizontal decalage to describe the gradual acquisition of conservation abilities.

Formal operational stage (11+ years): A person in the formal operational stage is able to think abstractly and is capable of hypothetico-deductive reasoning, which means that he can identify competing hypotheses about a problem and strategies for systematically testing those hypotheses. In adolescence, there is a renewed **egocentrism**, which now involves an inability to separate one's own abstract thoughts from the thoughts of others.

Research evaluating Piaget's theory has generally confirmed that cognitive development occurs in a predictable sequence of stages and that a stage is never skipped; however, cultural studies have suggested that the ages at which children reach each stage may vary.

2. Information Processing and Neo-Piagetian Theories: Information processing theories grew, in part, out of research comparing the functioning of computer programs to the human mind. These theories describe cognitive development as involving increasing information processing capacity and efficiency. From this perspective, cognitive abilities are similar at all stages of development but differ in terms of extent. For example, improvements in memory are due to increased memory capacity, enhanced processing speed, and greater automaticity. In contrast to Piagetians, information processing theorists focus on development within specific cognitive domains such as attention, memory, and reasoning, rather than on identifying global principles of development. They also view cognitive ability as task-specific and are more interested in how specific skills are used for particular tasks and contexts.

Neo-Piagetian theories combine the information processing and Piagetian approaches. Like Piaget, the neo-Piagetians recognize the roles of biological maturation and experience in cognitive development and propose that individuals actively construct their own knowledge. However, like information processing theorists, they focus more on developmental changes within specific cognitive domains and on the impact of the context in which development occurs. Consequently, they consider unevenness in development across domains and contexts as a normal part of development (Knight & Sutton, 2004).

3. Vygotsky's Sociocultural Theory: The Russian psychologist Vygotsky (1978) acknowledged the impact of biology on cognitive development but placed greater emphasis on the role of social and cultural factors. His sociocultural theory views all learning as socially mediated and proposes that cognitive development is first interpersonal (which refers to the child's interactions with others) and then intrapersonal (which occurs when the child internalizes what he has learned).

According to Vygotsky, cognitive development is facilitated when instruction and other environmental demands fall within the child's **zone of proximal development**, which refers to the discrepancy between a child's current developmental level (the level at which the child can function independently) and the level of development that is just beyond his current level but can be reached when an adult or more experienced peer provides appropriate scaffolding. **Scaffolding** refers to instruction, assistance, and support and is most effective when it involves modeling, providing cues, and encouraging the child to think about alternative plans of action. Vygotsky also proposed that symbolic (make-believe) play provides a child with a zone of proximal development that enables the child to practice behaviors in situations that require less precision and accuracy than would be required in reality.

Vygotsky noticed that young children often talk aloud to themselves when performing tasks. In contrast to Piaget, who referred to this speech as egocentric, Vygotsky described it as self-directed (private) speech that helps children regulate and organize their own behaviors. As children grow older, self-directed speech becomes internalized as inner (silent) speech.

Memory

1. Memory Processes: The acquisition and recall of memories involves three processes: (a) Encoding involves the translation of incoming stimuli into a code that can be processed by the brain. Although encoding is often automatic, it is more effective when it involves deliberate rehearsal. (b) Storage is the process of maintaining information in memory. Storage can be disrupted by several factors including interference and brain trauma. (c) Retrieval refers to the recovery of stored information. Retrieval is facilitated by the use of retrieval cues.

2. Components of Memory: The information processing model describes memory as consisting of three components:

Sensory memory (sensory register): Sensory memory seems to be capable of storing a great deal of information about sensory stimuli, but this information is retained for no more than a few seconds.

Short-term memory: Information in sensory memory is transferred to short-term memory (STM) when it becomes the focus of attention. Short-term memory holds a limited amount of information, and, without rehearsal, information in short-term memory begins to fade within 30 seconds. Short-term memory consists of *primary memory* (passive memory storage) and *working memory*. Working memory is responsible for the manipulation and processing of information (e.g., working memory allows you to repeat a phone number you just saw written down until you dial the number on the phone).

Long-term memory: Although the process involved in converting information from short-term memory to long-term memory (LTM) is not well understood, it is likely due to the type of rehearsal: Information is more likely to be transferred to long-term memory with elaborative rehearsal, which involves relating new information to existing information, than maintenance rehearsal, which involves simply repeating the new information with little or no interpretation. The capacity of long-term memory seems to be unlimited, and some experts believe that material stored in long-term memory is permanent. Long-term memory consists of *recent memory* (memory for information from the immediate past) and *remote memory* (memory for information from the distant past). Permanent memory is also called **secondary memory** – information stored in secondary memory can be recalled after hours, days, months, or years.

3. Types of Long-Term Memory: The major types of LTM include procedural memory, declarative memory, and prospective memory. *Procedural memory* stores information about how to do things ("learning how"). It is used to acquire, retain, and employ perceptual, cognitive, and motor skills and habits. Procedural memories are acquired through observation and practice and are difficult to forget. A second type of LTM, *declarative memory*, mediates the acquisition of facts ("learning that or what"). It is further subdivided into semantic and autobiographical (episodic) memory. *Semantic memory* includes knowledge about language, "common sense" knowledge, and information related to the rules of logic and inference. **Autobiographical (episodic) memory** stores information about events that have been personally experienced. Autobiographical memory is affected more by normal aging than semantic or procedural memory. Flashbulb memories (vivid, detailed images of what one was doing at the time a dramatic event occurred) are stored in autobiographical memory. Finally, *prospective memory* is the capacity to remember to do things in the future (i.e., to "remember to remember"). People can deliberately enhance their prospective memory by using external aides such as lists.

4. Memory in Early Childhood: Autobiographical (episodic) memory is generally inaccurate until after age 3, and its accuracy then increases gradually during the preschool years. This is one reason why interviewing young children requires an understanding of their cognitive abilities, including their encoding and retrieval skills.

Preschoolers' autobiographical memories are sometimes accurate. Most preschoolers can provide fairly accurate answers to open-ended questions about events they have experienced (e.g., "What was your favorite ride at Disneyland?") and can store emotionally vivid events (ones that made them happy, sad, or afraid) accurately in memory and even describe them afterwards (Stein, 1995). Preschoolers' memories fade faster than those of older children and adults, however, and, therefore, a key determinant of the accuracy of preschoolers' memories is how soon after an event they are interviewed.

Additionally, because preschoolers are more vulnerable to suggestion than older children and adults, their memories can be influenced more easily by other people's suggestions, including suggestions from adults who are asking them questions (especially **leading questions** and questions that are asked repeatedly). This is of concern when interviewing children and when children are asked to testify in court, such as in cases of suspected child abuse. The testimony of children, especially preschoolers, should be evaluated on a case-by-case basis.

Children's Understanding of Death and Time

1. Children's Understanding of Death: A realistic understanding of death develops during childhood and is related to both level of cognitive development and experience. Most young children (age 3 until age 5) don't understand that death is irreversible and believe that the dead retain some of the capacities they had while alive. Children age 5 to 9 know that death is universal and irreversible but tend to personify it (e.g., turn it into a "bogeyman"). By age 10, children understand that the end of life is a biological process and is not due to an outside force.

2. Children's Understanding of Time: Before age 5, children have very little understanding of the concept of time, the past, or the future. Without this understanding, they have difficulty imagining things they have not experienced and are unable to think logically about cause and effect. At about age 5 or 6, children begin to develop a sense of time and the ability to conceptualize cause and effect in a logical way. For example, they start to think about the likely outcomes of their behavior and are able to use their past experiences to imagine what these outcomes might be.

Cognitive Performance in Late Adulthood

Normal aging has an effect on the brain and its functions through a number of pathways (e.g., neurological changes, changes in blood flow to the brain); however, the extent to which these changes affect cognitive functioning varies from person to person. Additionally, for some older people, vision changes or hearing loss affect the quality of perception and the ability to receive, process, and react to information. One of the best predictors of the maintenance of cognitive functioning in late adulthood is physical health (Schaie & Hertzog, 1986), particularly cardiovascular health, which seems to have a direct impact on reaction time.

1. Memory Loss: A common cognitive change for older people is memory loss, often in the form of recall (e.g., recalling names, losing things). An older person's memory loss may be due, in part, to age-related declines in recent long-term memory, but there is evidence that it may also reflect age-related changes in metamemory (Sugar, 1989).

Additionally, certain medical conditions (e.g., cardiovascular problems, diabetes), depression, and some vitamin deficiencies and medications can impair memory function. In older people, temporary or reversible memory problems caused by these factors are sometimes misdiagnosed as dementia (dementia is called major neurocognitive disorder in the DSM-5; see the note below).

2. Mild Cognitive Impairment: Mild cognitive impairment (MCI) may be diagnosed when an older person has memory problems that are greater than those associated with normal aging but lacks the behavioral symptoms and functional impairment associated with dementia (Bennett, 2004). It is unknown whether MCI is a separate condition or an early sign of dementia, and patients and their families may have a hard time coping with the uncertainty about whether MCI will progress to dementia. (NOTE: In the DSM-5, the diagnosis of "major neurocognitive disorder" subsumes the DSM-IV-TR diagnosis of dementia and is diagnosed when there is evidence of *significant* decline from a previous level of functioning in one or more cognitive domains that interferes with the individual's independence in everyday activities. The DSM-5 also includes the diagnosis of "mild neurocognitive disorder," which subsumes the DSM-IV-TR diagnosis of cognitive disorder NOS and is the appropriate diagnosis when there is evidence of a *modest* decline from a previous level of functioning in one or more cognitive domains that does *not* interfere with the individual's independence in everyday activities but may require greater effort or compensatory strategies.)

D. Language Development and Acquisition

1. Theories of Language Development: The primary explanations for language development are provided by the nativist, behaviorist, and interactionist approaches. The nativist approach attributes language acquisition to biological mechanisms and stresses universal patterns of language development. Chomsky (1968), an advocate of this position, proposes that an innate **language acquisition device** (LAD) makes it possible for a person to acquire language just by being exposed to it. Support for this proposal comes from studies showing that children master the basics of language between the ages of 4 and 6 regardless of the complexity of their native language and that children from all cultures pass through the same stages of language development.

In contrast, the behaviorist approach proposes that language is acquired like any other behavior through imitation and reinforcement. In other words, children acquire language by observing and imitating the language of others and being reinforced for doing so.

Finally, **interactionists** believe language development is attributable to a combination of biological and environmental factors. The social-communications version of this approach stresses the impact of social interactions. For instance, in at least some cultures, adults seem to naturally use **child-directed speech** (which is also known as motherese and parentese) when speaking to very young children: They speak more slowly, use shorter and simpler sentences, exaggerate and repeat the most important words, and frequently ask questions. In addition, adults often respond to a child's communications with an expansion or extension: An adult is responding with an expansion when he adds to the child's statement but retains the child's word order (e.g., when a child says, "Mommy bye-bye" and his father responds, "Yes, Mommy is going bye-bye"). In contrast, an adult is responding with an extension when he adds information to the child's statement (e.g., when a child says, "Mommy bye-bye" and his father responds, "Yes, Mommy is going to work now").

2. Stages of Language Acquisition: Children in different cultures progress through similar stages of language acquisition. Throughout these stages, **receptive language** (comprehension) precedes **productive language**. In other words, preschool children can understand much of what is said to them before they can verbally express their own ideas.

Stage 1 – Crying: Infants initially produce three distinct patterns of crying: a basic (hunger) cry, an anger cry, and a pain cry. By 1 or 2 months of age, they also produce a fussy (irregular) cry.

Stage 2 – Cooing and babbling: Beginning at 6 to 8 weeks, infants produce simple "cooing" sounds that consist mainly of vowels and are usually emitted when the infant is happy and contented. This is followed, at about 4 months, by **babbling**, which involves the repetition of simple consonant and vowel sounds (e.g., "bi-bi-bi"). Early babbling includes sounds from all languages, but between 9 and 14 months, babies narrow their repertoire of sounds to those of their native language. Although early studies found that deaf children begin to babble at about the same age as hearing children, more recent research suggests that only deaf children with residual hearing resemble hearing children in terms of early verbalizations (Oller & Eilers, 1988). Interestingly, at about the same age at which hearing children begin to babble, deaf children begin to make repetitive, rhythmic gestures ("babble") with their hands (Pettito & Marentetto, 1991).

Stage 3 – Echolalia and expressive jargon: Beginning at about 9 months, children imitate adult speech sounds and words without an understanding of their meaning (**echolalia**). This is followed by vocalizations of sounds that resemble sentences but that, again, have no meaning (**expressive jargon**).

Stage 4 – First words: In infancy, receptive vocabulary exceeds productive vocabulary; and, by about 13 months of age, infants understand about 50 words. Most infants speak their **first word** between the ages of 10 and 15 months and, by 18 months, speak about 50 words. First words are most often nominals, or labels for objects, people, or events, although action words, modifiers, and personal-social words (e.g., please) also occur. Nominals are most likely to refer to dynamic objects (dog, car) or objects the child uses (spoon). For many children, the very first word is either "mama" or "dada." From 1 to 2 years of age, children use single words that express whole phrases and sentences. This is referred to as **holophrastic speech** and involves using gestures and intonation to turn a single word into a comment, question, or command.

Stage 5 – Telegraphic speech: By 18 to 24 months, children exhibit telegraphic speech – i.e., they string two or more words together to make a sentence (e.g., "me go"). While these phrases initially contain only nouns, verbs, and adjectives, by 27 months, prepositions and pronouns have been added. At this point, the child's vocabulary contains about 300 to 400 words.

Stage 6 – Vocabulary growth: At about 18 months, children begin to exhibit a rapid increase in vocabulary, with the fastest rate of growth occurring between 30 and 36 months. At 36 months, the child's vocabulary includes about 1,000 words, and his sentences often contain three or four words. By age 6, vocabulary will have increased to between 8,000 and 14,000 words.

Stage 7 – Grammatically correct sentences: The period from 2-1/2 to 5 years of age is marked by increasing sentence complexity, grammatical accuracy, and continued vocabulary growth, with about 50 new words being learned each month. The child also increasingly uses questions, negatives, and the passive voice. A temporary overgeneralization of grammatical rules is common during this period.

Stage 8 – Metalinguistic awareness: During the early school years, children gain metalinguistic awareness, or the ability to reflect on language as a communication tool and on themselves as language users. By age 6 or 7, for example, children recognize that words are different from the concepts they represent, and they can use words in humorous and metaphoric ways.

3. Childhood Speech Errors and Delays in Language Development: Although children develop speech in a predictable sequence, the amount of speech individual children have at age 2 can vary greatly: Some 2 year olds speak in two-word phrases, others speak in longer sentences, and both are normal.

a. Common Childhood Speech Errors: During the course of language development, it is common for children to exhibit underextensions and overextensions. Overextension occurs when a child applies a word to a wider collection of objects and events than is appropriate (e.g., the child calls all four-legged animals "dog"). Underextension occurs when a child uses a word in a narrower sense than adults do (e.g., a child might use the word "dish" only to refer to the plastic dish he uses).

Additionally, **speech dysfluencies** (i.e., stuttering, including sound repetitions, broken words, blocking, etc.) are common in preschool children (ages 2 to 4) and most outgrow them and develop normal speech without intervention.

b. Hearing-Impaired Children: It can be difficult to detect hearing problems in a baby because, as noted, deaf infants with residual hearing begin to babble at the same age that unimpaired infants do; these babies don't usually begin to show problems in learning language until about 9 months of age. Parents who don't know that their baby has a hearing problem may think he has intellectual disability. A way to identify a hearing problem in a baby is to observe how he responds to a sudden loud noise: The baby may have a hearing problem if he doesn't startle or look to find the source of the noise.

Early intervention for hearing impairment usually enhances development, and, if the problem is detected early, a baby can learn sign language in the same progression as he would have learned spoken language.

c. Inadequate Verbal Stimulation: To develop speech, infants need to hear spoken language. Parents who lack developmental information may neglect to interact verbally with their infant because they know he doesn't understand speech yet. Adolescent parents, in particular, need to be encouraged to speak to their baby. Another potential problem is parents who avoid talking to their baby using **child-directed speech**. The research suggests that hearing such "baby talk" is important for normal infant development and helps infants learn language better (Fernald, 1987).

E. Temperament and Family Influences on Personality

1. Temperament: Temperament refers to a person's basic disposition, which influences how he responds to and interacts with the environment. Temperament seems to be affected by heredity and is, to some degree, apparent at birth and predictive of later personality and adjustment.

a. Categories of Temperament: Thomas and Chess (1977; Chess & Thomas, 1987) distinguish between nine basic temperament qualities – activity level, rhythmicity, approach/withdrawal, adaptability, threshold of responsiveness, intensity of reaction, quality of mood, distractibility, and persistence – and propose that most babies can be categorized on the basis of these qualities as either "easy," "difficult," or "slow-to-warm-up."

- "Easy" children are even-tempered, have regular sleeping and eating patterns, adapt easily to new situations and people, and have a preponderance of positive moods.
- "Difficult" children are irritable, withdraw from new situations and people, and have unpredictable habits and a preponderance of negative moods.
- "Slow-to-warm-up" children are inactive and somewhat negative in mood and take time to adjust to new stimuli.

b. Goodness-of-Fit Model: Thomas and Chess found that many children categorized as "difficult" or "easy" at age 3 were rated, respectively, as poorly- or well-adjusted as young adults. However, the relationship between early temperament and later adjustment was not perfect, and, based on this finding, these investigators developed a **goodness-of-fit model**. This model predicts that it is the degree of match between parents' behaviors and the child's temperament that contributes to the child's outcomes.

Thomas and Chess and others have developed parent guidance interventions designed to help parents interact with their child in ways that are consistent with the child's temperament. Lieberman (1993), for example, recommends that the parents of a "slow-to-warm-up" child should introduce the child to new situations slowly – they should stay near him until he appears comfortable or is enjoying the situation and only then back away.

2. Family Influences on Personality:

a. Parenting Style: Baumrind (1991) has presented a framework for understanding the impact of parenting on development. Her approach combines two dimensions of parenting – responsivity (warmth) and demandingness (control) – to derive **four parenting styles**, which are predictive of specific personality and behavioral outcomes for children and adolescents.

> *Authoritarian:* Authoritarian parents exhibit high demandingness and low responsivity. They impose absolute standards of conduct, stress obedience, and use power assertive techniques (e.g., physical punishment, threats, and deprivation) to gain compliance. Their offspring are often irritable, aggressive, and dependent and have a limited sense of responsibility and low levels of self-esteem and academic achievement.
>
> *Authoritative:* Authoritative parents combine rational control with responsivity. Although they set clear rules and high standards for their children, they rely on inductive techniques (reasoning, praise, explanations) to gain compliance and encourage independence. The offspring of authoritative parents tend to be assertive, self-confident, socially responsible, and achievement-oriented and often obtain high grades in school.
>
> *Indulgent-permissive:* Indulgent-permissive parents are warm and caring but make few demands and are nonpunitive. Their offspring tend to be impulsive, self-centered, easily frustrated, and low in achievement and independence.
>
> *Rejecting-neglecting:* Rejecting-neglecting parents exhibit low levels of responsivity and demandingness, they minimize the time and effort they spend with their children, and they may be overtly hostile toward their children. Offspring of these parents have low self-esteem and are often impulsive, moody, and aggressive.

b. Family Composition: First-borns are usually more achievement-oriented and socially responsible. In contrast, later-borns are often less cautious, have better peer relationships, and are more confident in social situations (Mussen et al., 1980). A child's characteristics are also affected by family size and the spacing (number of years) between siblings. For example, the larger the family and the smaller the gap between children, the lower the children's achievement (Wagner et al., 1985; Zajonc, 1976).

F. Identity Development

1. Gender-Role Identity: Gender-role identity refers to a person's sense of being a male or female. The research has confirmed that gender-role identity is fairly well-established by age 3: Most 3 year olds label themselves as either a boy or a girl, classify others as being of the same or opposite sex, and know what behaviors are considered appropriate and inappropriate for a boy or girl.

a. Theories of Gender-Role Identity Development: Explanations for the development of gender-role identity include the following:

> *Psychodynamic theory:* According to Freud's psychodynamic theory, the development of gender-role identity depends on successful resolution of the psychosexual crisis of the phallic stage of development, which results in identification with the same-sex parent.

Social learning theory: Social learning theory predicts that children first acquire gender-typed behaviors through rewards and punishments (Mischel, 1966) and modeling and imitation (Bandura, 1969). Eventually, they develop a gender-role identity.

Cognitive development theory: According to Kohlberg's (1966) cognitive development theory, the acquisition of gender-role identity involves a sequence of stages that parallels cognitive development. By age 2 or 3, children recognize that they are either male or female (**gender identity**). Soon thereafter, children realize that gender identity is stable over time (**gender stability**) – boys grow up to be men and girls grow up to be women. By age 6 or 7, children understand that gender is constant over situations and know that people cannot change gender by superficially altering their external appearance or behavior (**gender constancy**).

Gender schema theory: Bem's (1981) gender schema theory attributes the acquisition of a gender-role identity to a combination of social learning and cognitive development. According to Bem, children develop "schemas" (conceptual frameworks) of masculinity and femininity as a result of their sociocultural experiences. These schemas then organize how the individual perceives and thinks about the world.

b. Gender-Role Identity and Adjustment: Hall and Halberstadt (1980) found that gender-role identity had a greater impact than biological sex on self-esteem. Their results indicated that, for both males and females, **androgyny** (which combines masculine and feminine characteristics and preferences) and, to a lesser degree, masculinity were both associated with higher levels of self-esteem than was femininity.

Sandra Bem (1993) found that androgynous people (people who scored high on both the masculine and feminine scales of her Sex Role Inventory) were better adjusted than sex-typed people and more flexible because they displayed either "masculine" behavior (e.g., rationality), "feminine" behavior (e.g., empathy), or a combination of the two, depending on the demands of the situation.

Although studies like these have suggested that androgyny is associated with positive characteristics, such as higher levels of self-esteem, achievement, and interpersonal satisfaction, other studies have not found androgynous people to be psychologically healthier than sex-typed people (Taylor & Hale, 1982).

c. Stability of Gender-Role Differences: While there may be some decline in gender-role differences in late adolescence and early adulthood, the distinction often reappears when adults marry. Even among "liberated" and dual-earner couples, the gender gap often widens when the first child is born and the woman assumes primary responsibility for child rearing and housekeeping (Cowan & Cowan, 1987; Gager, 1998). Beginning in middle-age, there may be some degree of gender-role reversal, with men becoming more passive, expressive, sensitive, and dependent and women becoming more active, outgoing, independent, and competitive (Huyck, 1990).

2. Racial/Ethnic Identity: Initial steps in adopting a racial/ethnic identity are recognizing the existence of racial differences and understanding the concept of race. Some studies suggest that infants may exhibit awareness of racial differences as early as 6 months of age and that children are able to label people in terms of racial group by the time they are 3 to 4 years old (e.g., Katz, 1976; Ramsey, 1995). However, a more sophisticated understanding of race does not develop until about age 10 when children begin to understand the social connotations of racial differences (e.g., Alejandro-Wright, 1985; Ramsey, 1995).

3. Adolescent "Identity Crisis": Erikson, who introduced the term "identity crisis," considered the primary developmental task of adolescence to be the achievement of a coherent identity.

a. Identity Statuses: Erikson's view was expanded by Marcia (1987), who distinguishes between four identity statuses (patterns) that reflect the degree to which the adolescent has experienced (or is experiencing) an identity crisis and is committed to an identity.

> *Identity diffusion:* The adolescent has not yet experienced an identity crisis or explored alternatives and is not committed to an identity.
>
> *Identity foreclosure:* The adolescent has not experienced a crisis but has adopted an identity (occupation, ideology, etc.) that has been imposed by others (often the same-sex parent).
>
> *Identity moratorium:* The adolescent experiences an identity crisis and actively explores alternative identities. During this period, an adolescent exhibits a high degree of confusion, discontent, and rebelliousness.
>
> *Identity achievement:* Adolescents who have resolved the identity crisis by evaluating alternatives and committing to an identity are "identity achieved."

b. Resolution of the Adolescent "Identity Crisis": The typical adolescent "identity crisis" is partially resolved by the shift from dependence to increasing independence. Strategies used in early childhood to achieve separation may return during this period – i.e., for many adolescents negativism (resistance to any form of control) reflects a renewed effort to achieve independence.

Parent factors associated with successful adolescent identity formation include a willingness to negotiate with their adolescent child, providing the child with support and reassurance, allowing the child to establish his own point of view, and a family atmosphere that promotes **individuation** (Hauser et al., 1987). (An adolescent individuates when he learns to see himself as differentiated from others, including his family.)

c. Gilligan's Relational Crisis for Girls: Gilligan found that at about 11 or 12 years of age, girls experience a relational crisis in response to increasing pressure to fit cultural stereotypes about the "perfect good woman" (1991, p. 22). As a result, they disconnect from themselves in order to maintain relationships with others. Consequences of this crisis include a drop in academic achievement, a loss of self-esteem, and an increased vulnerability to psychological problems. Gilligan proposes that males experience a similar relational crisis but do so in early childhood rather than adolescence.

G. Development of Self-Awareness and Self-Concept

"Self-awareness" refers to an individual's understanding that he is separate from others, while "self-concept" is an individual's conscious cognitive perception and evaluation of himself. Self-concept starts to develop in early childhood, but experiences in adolescence also have a strong influence, and experiences in adulthood may lead a person to re-evaluate and change his self-concept. Additionally, every person has multiple self-concepts, and the one that is activated depends, to some extent, on what situation or task is most important at the time. A person's self-concept affects his social functioning because how he responds to people and events is heavily influenced by what he thinks and feels about himself. Finally, because core beliefs affect the meanings that people assign to their lives and experiences, self-concept is also an element of spirituality.

1. Self-Awareness in Childhood and Adolescence: Self-awareness becomes apparent during the second year of life. According to Stipek and colleagues (1990), the development of self-awareness involves three stages:

- Physical self-recognition is evident by about 18 months of age when infants begin to recognize themselves in pictures and mirrors. According to Gergely, this mirror recognition requires certain cognitive skills, including the ability to construct "a visual feature representation of the typical physical appearance of not-directly visible parts of ... [one's own] body" (1994, p. 55).

- Self-description emerges between 19 and 30 months of age, when children use both neutral terms (e.g., "brown hair") and evaluative terms (e.g., "good girl") to describe themselves.

- Children subsequently exhibit emotional responses to wrongdoing, which means that they have adverse reactions to a caregiver's disapproval. Stipek et al. conclude this reaction signals the beginning of the development of a sense of conscience.

Self-awareness undergoes predictable changes during childhood and adolescence, and these changes are reflected in how youngsters describe themselves (Damon & Hart, 1988; Harter, 1988): From ages 2 to 6, self-descriptions focus on concrete physical characteristics, specific behaviors, and preferences (e.g., "I'm a girl," "I like to ride my bike"). In middle childhood (ages 6 to 10), children's self-descriptions often refer to competencies (e.g., "I'm a very good soccer player but I'm not very good at math"); and toward the end of middle childhood (ages 10 to 12), youngsters often describe themselves in terms personality traits ("I'm popular," "I'm shy") and emotions directed toward themselves (e.g., "I'd be ashamed of myself if I failed the test"). Finally, adolescents describe themselves more abstractly, using terms that refer to their inner thoughts and feelings (e.g., "I'm moody, sensitive, and a total introvert"), and they recognize that their attributes are sometimes inconsistent ("I'm usually sensitive about other people's feelings, but sometimes I say horrible things to my friends and family members").

2. Self-Concept in Adolescence: Adolescents are concerned about their physical appearance and how others perceive how they look. Self-esteem appears to be at its lowest point during early adolescence (ages 12 to 14), when teens are extremely self-conscious and their perceptions of themselves are more easily influenced by others (Kaplan, 2004). Self-esteem in adolescence is also connected to how adolescents perceive their ability to meet short-terms goals. While adults better understand the lesson of not being the best at everything, adolescents struggle to understand this and sometimes see these failures as significant discrepancies.

Adolescence is marked by a renewed **egocentrism**, which is manifested in two ways (Elkind, 1967):

Imaginary audience: Adolescents often feel as though others are watching or paying attention to them (i.e., as though they are "on stage"). This accounts for their extreme self-consciousness.

Personal fable: Adolescents believe deeply in the uniqueness of their own experiences. This produces a sense of immortality and invulnerability to harm.

3. Self-Concept in Late Adulthood: For most people, old age includes the loss of roles and relationships that helped define their personal identity. As a result, older people often think about important roles, events, and people from their past. Such **reminiscence** is useful for helping them maintain a sense of self and for giving meaning to what they have done with their lives. As an intervention, reminiscence is designed to help older adults recall positive memories from the past in order to improve their mood. Social workers often incorporate an older client's desire to reminisce into the intervention process.

Body Image

Body image is "the perception that a person has of their physical self and the thoughts and feelings that result from that perception. These feelings can be positive, negative or both and are influenced by individual and environmental factors" (National Eating Disorders Collaboration). According to the National Eating Disorders Collaboration, there are four aspects to body image:

Perceptual: How you see your body (which may or may not correlate to how your body actually looks)

Affective: How you feel about your body (related to satisfaction or dissatisfaction with shape, weight, specific body parts, etc.

Cognitive: The way you think about your body (can lead to preoccupation with thoughts about your body

Behavioral: Behaviors in which you engage as a result of your body image (for example, excessive exercising, disordered eating, etc.

Individuals experiencing body dissatisfaction may also experience eating disorders and other mental health consequences. Body image disproportionately affects women - research has shown that nearly half of all women feel negatively about their bodies, and poor body image has been linked to negative outcomes for mental, sexual and physical health (Ramseyer Winter et al., 2017). Poor body image is linked to poor self-esteem, and some research has indicated that it is caused by sociocultural influences including pressure from family, friends and the media. It may lead an individual to experience damaging levels of body dissatisfaction, or to engage in disordered eating or other excessive efforts to alter her body (Fenton et al., 2010).

Risk factors associated with poor body image include: *low self-esteem, socioeconomic status, low self-confidence, and general health concerns* (Fenton et al., 2010). However, it may be more helpful for practitioners to focus on more positive, or protective factors in treating clients who suffer from poor body image. A clinician using an assets-based approach will focus on attributes of clients that help them to cope. For body image, some particularly helpful assets may include social competence, adaptability, problem solving skills, autonomy, a sense of purpose and an awareness of the future (Fenton et al., 2010).

Body image dissatisfaction is often treated with cognitive-behavioral therapy (CBT). Clinicians help clients determine the factors that contribute to their poor body image, helping them to adjust their thought process and behaviors. Some questions a CBT practitioner might ask a client facing negative body image are as follows: "Are you worried about your appearance in any way? What aspects of your appearance do you dislike? How much distress do these concerns cause you? Do your concerns interrupt other areas of your life?" (Gibson, 2015). However, it is important to consider that broader cultural and societal factors contribute to clients' body image dissatisfaction. Some researchers have suggested that a therapeutic approach encouraging clients to question society's expectations for their bodies may be an empowering alternative strategy that broadens the problem from the individual to a cultural one (Gibson, 2015).

H. Attachment

Attachment refers to the strong emotional bond that develops between an infant and his primary caregiver. To form an attachment, an infant needs consistent care from a person who is reliable and predictable. This person may be the biological mother, biological father, grandmother, adoptive parent, etc. An infant who receives consistent care from more than one person can form multiple attachments (Bremmer, 1988). The time right after birth is not the only opportunity for developing attachment. The mothers of adopted babies or premature infants who spend time in the hospital after birth also form attachments with their children (Ashford et al., 2006).

1. Theories of Attachment: Psychoanalytic theory describes the attachment of an infant to his mother as the consequence of oral gratification, while learning theory regards it as the result of reinforcement (i.e., infants develop attachments to people who provide them with food, affection, and other pleasurable experiences). Of these two theories, **learning theory** has received the most support. For example, infant rhesus monkeys in Harlow's research were raised with two surrogate mothers, a wire-mesh mother and a terrycloth mother. Regardless of which mother provided food, the infants became "attached" to the terrycloth mother. Harlow concluded that a baby's attachment to his mother is due, in part, to **contact comfort**, or the pleasant tactile sensation that is provided by a soft, cuddly parent (Harlow & Harlow, 1969).

An alternative approach is provided by ethological theory, which proposes that humans have a biological tendency to form attachments because they help guarantee an infant's survival. Ethological theory originated from studies with animals, which found that the critical period for **imprinting** in geese is during the first two or three days after birth (Lorenz, 1965). These studies found that newly hatched chicks follow the first moving object they see during this period (which is usually their mother); but, if they are not exposed to a moving object, imprinting does not occur.

Bowlby (1980) applied the notion of critical period to human attachment and proposed that exposure of an infant to his mother during this period results in a bond between them. He believed that humans are born with a biological predisposition that increases the likelihood that attachments will form: Infants are programmed to cry, smile, and vocalize in order to get a caregiver's attention, protection, and love, while adults are programmed to respond to an infant's behaviors. Bowlby distinguished between four stages of attachment development that occur during the first two years of life – preattachment, attachment-in-the-making, clearcut attachment, and the formation of reciprocal relationships. According to Bowlby, as a result of experiences during these stages, a child develops an "internal working model," which is a mental representation of self and others that influences the child's future relationships.

2. Signs of Attachment: During the first few months of life, infants emit attachment behaviors indiscriminately but, by 6 to 7 months of age, these behaviors become increasingly directed toward the primary caregiver(s). Signs of attachment include the following:

Social referencing: By about 6 months of age, infants begin to look to their caregiver to determine how to respond in new or ambiguous situations.

Separation anxiety: **Separation anxiety** refers to severe distress that occurs when a child is separated from his primary caregiver. It begins at about 6 to 8 months of age, is most intense at 14 to 18 months, and then gradually declines. Unlike separation anxiety disorder (a disorder in the DSM-5), anxiety about separation during this developmental period is considered normal. It reflects the young child's increasing cognitive abilities (e.g., the child recognizes that his caregiver is leaving and wonders why and when she will return) and growing emotional and social bonds with his primary caregiver.

Stranger anxiety: By about 8 to 10 months, infants become very anxious and fearful in the presence of a stranger, especially when a caregiver is not nearby or when the caregiver does not respond positively to the stranger. **Stranger anxiety** continues until about age 2 and then diminishes.

3. Patterns of Attachment: To study attachment, Ainsworth and colleagues (1978) devised the "**Strange Situation**," which involves several phases during which the mother leaves her infant alone in a room with a stranger and then returns. Research using this technique has identified four distinct patterns of attachment:

Secure attachment: A securely attached infant is mildly upset by his mother's absence and actively seeks contact with her when she returns. Mothers of securely attached children are emotionally sensitive and responsive to their babies' cues. A secure attachment pattern is more likely to develop when a mother has an adequate social support network.

Insecure (anxious)/ambivalent attachment: A baby exhibiting this attachment pattern becomes very disturbed when left alone with a stranger but is ambivalent when his mother returns and may become angry and resist her attempts at physical contact. Mothers of these children are often moody and inconsistent in their caregiving (i.e., sometimes indifferent, at other times enthusiastic). This pattern is also referred to as insecure/resistant attachment.

Insecure (anxious)/avoidant attachment: An avoidant baby shows little distress when his mother leaves the room and avoids or ignores her when she returns. Mothers of avoidant children are very impatient and unresponsive or, at the other extreme, provide their children with too much stimulation.

Disorganized/disoriented attachment: A baby with this type of attachment (Main & Solomon, 1986) exhibits fear of his caregiver, dazed or confused facial expressions, and other disorganized attachment behaviors (e.g., greeting his mother when she returns but then turning away from her). This pattern is often found in children from families with unsupportive marital relationships, high levels of environmental stress, low levels of social support, and other problems that interfere with the mother's ability to interact with her infant. About 80 percent of infants who have been mistreated by their caregivers exhibit this pattern (Carlson et al., 1989).

The effects of insecure attachment are not always predictable. While some insecurely attached children have later adjustment problems, others do not; and there is evidence that the impact of insecure attachment is related to continuity of care – i.e., insecurely attached infants are less likely to develop adjustment problems when their parents' caregiving skills improve and/or when they develop strong bonds to individuals outside the immediate family (e.g., NICHD Early Child Care Research Network, 2006).

4. Attachment to Fathers: Infants form attachments to their fathers even when their mothers are the primary caregivers, and children usually exhibit similar types of attachment to both parents (Fox et al., 1991). However, the types of interactions that lead to attachment center more around play activities for fathers but on nurturance and caregiving for mothers (Collins & Gunnar, 1990).

5. Factors That May Interfere With Attachment: The following factors have the potential to interfere with the mother-infant relationship and attachment (Ashford et al., 2006):

Infant-related factors: Premature infants are less responsive than typical full-term infants and often spend time in the neonatal intensive care unit, where interacting with their mother (and father) is difficult. Attachment, however, usually develops once the mother takes the infant home, and attachment patterns of premature and full-term infants are essentially the same (Wintgens et al., 1998). Other infant-related factors that can interfere with attachment include drug exposure and difficult temperament.

Maternal factors: Depressed mothers may not be responsive to their babies and may overlook their social cues, often because they are preoccupied with their own painful feelings. In addition, a baby will tend to take on his mother's mood. Other parental factors that can interfere with attachment include alcoholism or drug abuse, childhood abuse and neglect, and adolescent motherhood. Adolescent mothers tend to talk less to their babies and may have trouble interpreting their cues and responding in appropriate ways (Hann et al., 1990).

Factors in the home: Home factors affecting attachment include the presence of many young children in the home (the mother may not have time to respond adequately to her new infant); low levels of support from the partner (a mother with a supportive partner tends to be more responsive to her infant); inadequate social support; and high levels of environmental stress. Dealing with poverty, domestic violence, or other chronic stressors may leave a mother too emotionally drained to interact consistently with her infant (Ashford et al., 2006; Crnic, 1984).

6. Prolonged Caregiver-Child Separation: Generally, early institutionalization of an infant appears to have the most negative impact when separation of the mother and baby occurs during the second half of the first year of life. In this situation, the infant may develop anaclitic depression, which is defined below. With an adequate, loving environment, appropriate intervention, and stable care, however, children can recover from early loss and deprivation (Emde, 1987). In addition, babies separated from caregivers do better if they are placed in a family-like environment.

a. Stages of Reaction to Prolonged Separation (Bowlby): **Bowlby** (1973) found that young children's reactions to prolonged separation from their primary caregiver involve three ordered stages:

Protest – the child refuses to accept the separation and responds by crying, kicking, etc.

Despair – the child appears to give up hope and becomes quiet, inactive, and withdrawn.

Detachment – if the separation continues, the child begins to accept attention from others, seems less unhappy, and may react with disinterest when the caregiver visits.

b. Anaclitic Depression: In a study of children placed in orphanages, Spitz (1945) found that babies who received adequate physical and medical care but little social interaction developed **anaclitic depression**, a syndrome involving developmental delays, unresponsiveness, and withdrawal. Severe cases of anaclitic depression are referred to as "hospitalism."

c. Preparing Children for Separation: Babies and children tolerate separations from their caregivers better if they are prepared for the separation in advance. Children should be given developmentally appropriate information about an upcoming separation and be told that they may feel afraid, lonely, and sad. Additionally, spending short periods of time away from the caregiver (e.g., at a relative's house) can help a child cope better with a later, more enduring separation (Stacey et al., 1970).

I. Communication

1. Gender and Communication Style: During childhood, the language of boys and girls reflects their preferred interactions: Boys rely more on language strategies that establish dominance, gain attention, and involve giving orders, while girls are more likely to use language that provides support, seeks common ground, and demonstrates attentiveness. In adolescence, boys tend to talk more in terms of competitive conversation, comparing knowledge and experience, while girls talk more about themselves, their personal feelings, and their relationships.

Among adults, men tend to prefer discussions about activities and events, while women usually prefer discussions about their personal lives, intimate topics, and feelings. Consequently, women tend to obtain a greater level of intimate communication with each other than men do. Additionally, men tend to use an **instrumental style** of communication, while women often use an **expressive style**. Instrumental communication focuses on identifying goals and solutions, while expressive communication emphasizes the expression of emotions and adopting a perspective that is sensitive to how others are feeling. Finally, in mixed-sex conversations, women are more often listeners and men are more often lecturers.

2. Bilingualism: The results of a number of early studies implied that bilingualism leads to cognitive deficits, but subsequent, better-controlled research found that bilingual children actually do as well as, or even better than, monolingual children on tests measuring both cognitive and language development (Diaz, 1983). There is some evidence, however, that these benefits are temporary and that, by adolescence, bilingual and monolingual speakers are indistinguishable in terms of these characteristics (Hakuta, 1987).

Among bilinguals, **code-switching** is common. This involves alternating between languages during a conversation and appears to serve several functions. For example, a bilingual speaker may switch from English to his native language to better express himself, establish rapport with the listener, or more effectively express his attitude toward the listener.

3. Ebonics (Black English or Black English Vernacular): Ebonics is a dialect of American English spoken in many African-American communities. Compared to standard English, Ebonics uses changes in pronunciation, distinctive slang, and different tenses. A person who speaks in this dialect will speak differently from a typical middle-class white person, but, within the context of his dialect, he will be using appropriate grammatical sentences and expressing himself in a clear and logical way.

4. The Deaf and Hard of Hearing: People born deaf constitute a small percentage of the hearing-impaired population, and social workers should be aware that are differences between people born deaf (the "culturally deaf") and people with hearing loss:

The "culturally deaf": Many people who are profoundly deaf were born deaf. These individuals have a community and a culture of their own, probably know how to use sign language (e.g., **American Sign Language**, or ASL), and tend to perceive deafness as an alternative lifestyle and culture rather than as a disability.

People with hearing loss: People who become hearing impaired usually miss the ability to hear, often perceive deafness as a loss, and, compared to the culturally deaf, are more likely to view deafness as a disability. People with hearing loss may withdraw from social contact as their ability to communicate with others changes and they lose their personal and cultural connections to the hearing world. Some people with hearing loss can **speech-read** (discern meaning from bits of sound and visual cues, such as lip movements), and people with hearing loss may also use amplifying devices. Speech-reading is only partially accurate, however, and can be very tiring.

5. Adults Who Are Illiterate: Adults are considered "functionally illiterate" when they cannot read, write, or perform arithmetic well enough to participate fully in society. Some adults who are illiterate have difficulty functioning independently. Illiteracy primarily affects people who belong to a minority group, were raised in socioeconomically disadvantaged communities, and/or are uneducated or undereducated (e.g., they completed high school but didn't learn basic literacy skills). In addition, some adults with disabilities are illiterate because they didn't receive encouragement at home or appropriate educational services at school.

Many adults who are illiterate are embarrassed by their inability to read or write and worry that others will discover their limitations. As a result, they hide their illiteracy from others and fail to seek help in learning to read and write. In addition, people who lack the ability to read street signs, newspapers, etc., may feel alienated from their community and may become angry, frustrated, or depressed as a result.

6. Non-English-Speaking Adults: Adults in the U.S. who do not speak English encounter some of the same difficulties as adults who are illiterate. Moreover, an immigrant's inability to communicate in English may force him into a low-paying job and ultimately into poverty, even if he is well educated. A non-English-speaking adult who depends on others to translate for him may encounter problems in his relationships. In addition, he may feel isolated if his inability to communicate with others in certain settings means that he has to keep his observations, ideas, feelings, etc., to himself.

7. Communication in Late Adulthood: An older adult's communication may be affected by sensory impairments, such as the loss of some ability to hear or see, or by cognitive impairments or depression. Very old people, even those without sensory or cognitive impairments, tend to speak more slowly and may take longer to respond in conversation.

"Elderspeak" is a way of speaking to older adults to facilitate their understanding. Its characteristics include using an exaggerated voice pitch and intonation, limited vocabulary, and simplified grammar, and speaking more slowly. Although research has found that elderspeak facilitates comprehension for some older people (Kemper & Mitzner, 2001), it may have the unwanted effect of undermining an older adult's self-esteem.

Finally, older adults with dementia benefit from being engaged in conversation. **Validation therapy** is an approach that emphasizes listening empathically to the feelings expressed by an older person with dementia, attempting to understand his feelings and needs through questioning, and accepting his view of reality rather than trying to reorient him to the present.

J. Emotional Growth and Development

Researchers (e.g., Ekman, 1993) have identified six basic emotions that are associated with the same facial expressions in a variety of cultures and are believed to be innate and universal – fear, anger, happiness, disgust, surprise, and sadness.

1. Emotional Development in Infancy and Toddlerhood:

a. Early Emotions: The research suggests that babies all over the world develop emotions at the same ages and in the same sequence (Izard et al., 1982). *Primary (basic) emotions* emerge first: Soon after birth, infants express interest, sadness, disgust, and distress through their facial expressions; and by 6 to 8 months, they also express anger, joy, surprise, and fear. It is not until the second year of life that children begin to display *self-conscious emotions*, which reflect children's ability to use social standards and rules to evaluate their own behaviors: At 18 to 24 months, they begin to show outward signs of jealousy, empathy, and embarrassment; and at 30 to 36 months, shame, guilt, and pride are also apparent (Lewis, 2002).

The ability of infants to detect emotions in others is manifested as *emotional contagion*, which appears during the first few weeks of life and occurs when an infant spontaneously cries in response to the cries of another infant (Eisenberg, 1992). Another early sign is the infant's reaction to the facial expressions of caregivers. For example, by about three months of age, infants imitate the sad, happy, and angry expressions of their caregivers (e.g., Haviland & Lelwica, 1987).

b. Smiling: Reflexive smiles are present from birth and result from internal stimuli, usually gas or other digestive processes. These smiles are most often seen while infants are sleeping in the first month following birth. **Social smiles** ("real" smiles), in contrast, occur as a result of external stimuli. Young infants most commonly smile when presented with a person's face, as opposed to a toy or an image on television. Social smiles can happen as early as 4 weeks of age, and a baby usually first smiles as a result of his caregiver's voice, face, or touch. By 6 months of age, babies become more selective in smiling. Six-month-old babies typically smile more for familiar caregivers than for strangers.

c. Social Referencing: Social referencing includes looking to others for emotional information. Babies as young as age 6 months can be affected by the moods of other people.

For example, babies of depressed mothers exhibit less play and exploratory behavior than babies of nondepressed mothers (Termine, 1988). By age 1, babies also look to strangers for cues on how to respond.

d. Emotional Regulation: The so-called "terrible 2s" result from a toddler's desire to establish his independence and sense of self-mastery (see also Erikson's theory of psychosocial development in Section I of this chapter). Social workers can explain this to parents as a way of normalizing a toddler's outwardly defiant behavior. Even preschool children, however, are capable of learning emotional language, cognitive strategies, and problem-solving to assist them in better understanding and regulating their emotions in emotional situations.

e. Fears: When preschoolers acquire the capacity for symbolic thought, they become more capable of using their imaginations, and one result of this is that they may develop fears, nightmares, or night terrors. Sometimes children's nightmares express feelings that they control in response to their fears while awake. Preschool and school-aged children can benefit from assistance in learning how to handle their negative feelings and frightening thoughts in adaptive ways. Useful approaches include teaching children how to talk about their feelings and reassuring them about their fears and other intense emotional reactions.

2. Emotional Development in Middle Childhood: Emotional development in interpersonal situations becomes important in middle childhood. Some school-age children are perceived as more irritable than they were before, while others become uncomfortable with their emotions when interacting with peers (some become embarrassed, others fear rejection).

a. Emotional Competence: A key task in middle childhood is the development of **emotional competence**, which refers to the ability to experience, express, and understand emotions – for instance, an "emotionally competent" child would be able to regulate his anger when he is punished (Denham et al., 2002): (a) A child who can "experience" emotions is aware of and recognizes his emotions and can regulate their expression. (b) Competence with emotional "expressiveness" means that the child can express his emotions in a way that is socially appropriate to the situation. (c) The ability to "understand" emotions allows the child to read other people's emotions so that he is able to respond appropriately. Additionally, the child understands that people have different emotional styles.

b. Internalizing and Externalizing Disorders: Most childhood (and adolescent) disorders can be described as either externalizing problems or internalizing problems (Achenbach & Edelbrock, 1983). **Externalizing problems** reflect issues of undercontrol. They consist of behaviors that reflect a tendency to act out. Examples include hyperactivity and acting defiantly or aggressively. **Internalizing problems** reflect issues of overcontrol and are believed to reflect the child's inner state. Examples include depression, anxiety, loneliness, and social withdrawal. Two of the most common problems in middle childhood are attention-deficit/hyperactivity disorder (an externalizing problem) and depression (an internalizing problem).

3. Emotional Development in Adolescence: A critical task for adolescents is learning how to cope with rapidly changing moods, particularly periods of feeling "down." To avoid becoming overwhelmed by their feelings, adolescents need to learn skills to cope with feeling sad, bored, etc., and may need help in gaining a better balance and perspective. For instance, because they may respond to boredom by engaging in unproductive activities, teenagers should be encouraged to take part in activities that allow them to experience feelings of personal fulfillment.

Examples of problems in adolescence are conduct disorder or delinquency (externalizing problems) and depression (an internalizing problem). Minor delinquent acts during adolescence are fairly common and usually not a sign of pathology; such acts often are motivated by a desire to be liked by peers or a wish to increase one's self-esteem. Below, we discuss delinquency and cutting. Other childhood and adolescent disorders and problems are discussed in your chapters covering Assessment and Interventions with Clients/Client Systems.

a. Delinquency: The term **delinquency** is used when a child or adolescent engages in illegal activities. The research has found that parental lack of supervision and inconsistent (or harsh) punishment are highly correlated with adolescent delinquency and involvement with antisocial friends (Dishion et al., 1991; Patterson et al., 1989). Research also shows that young children identified as aggressive have a high probability of becoming "delinquents" in adolescence (Loeber & Farrington, 2001). Other risk factors for delinquency include male gender; low school expectations; low attachment to school; low achievement in school; poor verbal ability; poor school conditions (rundown school, poor monitoring); low income status; living in a rundown neighborhood with a high crime rate; living in a dense urban community; and a family history of incarceration, violence, substance abuse, and/or mental illness (Dryfoos, 1990; Loeber & Farrington, 2001).

The best predictor of **recidivism**, or re-offense, is the person's age at first offense: The younger the person is when he commits his first crime, the higher the risk for recidivism. Thus, compared to juvenile (adolescent) offenders, child offenders have a greater risk of becoming serious and chronic offenders.

b. Self-Harm and Cutting: Behaviors involving self-harm (or self-mutilation) often have an onset in adolescence. These behaviors have been defined as "the deliberate destruction or alteration of one's own body tissue without conscious suicidal intent" (Favazza, 1987, p. 225). Self-harm has been associated with experiencing physical or sexual abuse, difficulties with impulse control, peer conflicts, exposure to alcoholism and violence, compulsive disorders, and eating and body image disorders. **Cutting** and other forms of self-mutilation are usually performed in secret, can take on an addictive quality, and typically evoke strong feelings in the person (e.g., shame, guilt).

Although the reasons for self-harm vary from person to person, many experts believe that the behavior may be used as a means of emotional expression and control. That is, self-harm may be used to provide relief from feelings, to prevent dissociation, to elicit euphoric feelings, to express pain, as a method of coping, as a form of communicating with other people, for self-nurturing or self-punishment, to re-enact experiences of being abused, and/or as a way of establishing emotional control (Alderman, 1997).

4. Emotional Development and Experience in Young Adulthood: A major developmental task for young adults is developing the ability to form intimate relationships. Young adults who do not develop this capacity experience **isolation** (the inability to share intimately with others), which can lead to a sense of **loneliness**. Loneliness is a subjective feeling in which a person has fewer interpersonal relationships than he wants or doesn't attain the level of personal satisfaction from interpersonal relationships that he desires. It differs from social isolation or spending time alone: Someone can have many friendships and still feel lonely; by contrast, another person may prefer spending time alone and desire few personal relationships.

Certain cognitions can cause an individual to avoid relationships and feel lonely as a result. Examples include the following: he feels undesirable or uninteresting; he feels unable to communicate with others or to get what he wants from relationships; he believes that he can't enjoy sex or can't perform well as a sexual partner; he fears he will embarrass himself; or he fears being hurt or is convinced he will ruin relationships (Young, 1982).

5. Emotional Development and Experience in Middle Adulthood:

a. Midlife Crisis and Self-Reflection: Although studies generally show that only a minority of adults experience a true "midlife crisis," many midlife men and women do engage in fairly intense self-reflection. For example, midlife adults often question whether they have led a meaningful life, and such reflection often influences the decisions and actions they take during this life period.

b. Well-Being and Anxiety: Well-being results from a psychological and emotional capacity to cope with demands over time and in different settings and situations. In middle adulthood, a person's well-being may be disrupted by fears and anxiety, which are common among both men and women during this period (Dziegielewski et al., 2002). Adults at midlife tend to fear one or more of the following: the process of aging and potential for loss of their mental and physical abilities; death; losing their sense of desirability (women); losing their sexual prowess (men); being alone in their later years; being undervalued at work; and losing their professional abilities and their jobs. For some adults, these fears can lead to anxiety.

c. Forgiveness: Most people by midlife have been hurt by loved ones (family, friends), and some may be struggling with the process of forgiveness. Many midlife adults have also hurt loved ones and not asked for forgiveness. Enright (2001) has identified a four-stage forgiveness process that can be used to help adults forgive others: uncover anger, decide to forgive, work on forgiveness, and discovery and release. This process requires the person to make significant changes in his feelings, perception of himself, and perspective about the causes of events in his life. Forgiveness differs from reconciliation because the latter also requires a change in the person who did the harm.

Forgiveness is associated with better mental health (lowered anxiety, depression, and hostility and increased hope, self-esteem, and existential well-being), as well as with improved physical health (anger and hostility are associated with health problems) (Ashford et al., 2006).

6. Emotional Development and Experience in Late Adulthood

a. "Integrity": Erikson characterized the final stage of the life-cycle as a conflict between integrity and despair. In this period, older people have an opportunity to integrate all aspects of their lives. An older person with unresolved issues from an earlier life stage may have difficulty dealing successfully with the last stage of life. For example, for some older people, threats to their autonomy may restimulate old feelings of shame.

b. Loss: Losses associated with late adulthood can compound over time and affect all areas of an older person's life, including his emotional well-being. Examples of these losses include retirement, death of loved ones, isolation from social contacts, declining physical health or cognitive functioning, reduced financial security, diminished feelings of independence, or the loss of familiar surroundings after placement. Some older adults experience fear or a sense of helplessness as a result of their losses. Additionally, the values, needs, and goals of some older adults don't match their circumstances. For example, an older person's activities may be more limited than he wants because of declines in his physical health.

c. Depression: The losses that accompany old age can sometimes lead to depression. For some older people, previously adequate defenses no longer enable them to regain their equilibrium and they become overwhelmed by their losses. Other older adults never had adequate defenses or emotional resources to deal with loss. For some older individuals, unresolved grief (e.g., over the loss of a spouse) can result in physical illness, depression, and an inability to form new relationships or build a new life.

Contrary to popular belief, however, healthy older adults are *not* at high risk for depression, and what may seem to be age-related depression in older people is usually depression about physical problems (Sue & Sue, 2003). In other words, in the absence of health problems, growing older does not increase the risk for depression, and, overall, older adults have lower rates of depressive disorders than younger adults.

d. Loneliness: An older adult may be lonely as a result of age-related losses or transitions (e.g., widowhood, moving to a new residence, a decline in health that limits activity). The risk for loneliness in late adulthood is highest for females, those over age 80, and those who have lower incomes. Sometimes loneliness is a precursor to or symptom of depression (Pinquart & Sorensen, 2001).

e. Spirituality and Religious Beliefs: Religious beliefs often increase after about age 60 (Hooyman & Kiyak, 2002). The sense of meaning that comes from spirituality or religious beliefs is associated with greater subjective well-being in older adults (Krause, 2003) and a better ability to come to terms with the inevitability of death. (For more information on spirituality, see Assessment, Section II.)

7. Emotional Intelligence: Emotional intelligence (EQ) refers to characteristics such as self-awareness, emotional understanding and regulation, ability to delay gratification, ability to channel emotions in the service of a goal (motivation), and having empathy for the feelings of others. EQ is not measured by intelligence tests, but recent research has found that it influences achievement and success in academic, social, and other settings. For instance, EQ affects how a person is able to use his cognitive abilities (e.g., a person's ability to regulate the effects of stress affects his concentration and problem-solving).

8. Emotions and Attitudes About Death and Dying:

a. Anxiety About Death: Although older individuals think about death more often than younger ones, anxiety about death seems to be greatest among middle-aged people (Gesser et al., 1987-88). Overall, anxiety about death is lower among better-adjusted people (e.g., those with high self-esteem, a sense of mastery, and a sense of purpose).

b. Kubler-Ross's Theory of Death and Dying: **Kubler-Ross** (1969) developed a theory of death and dying that describes the stages people go through as they move toward their own death. These stages include the following:

Stage 1 – Denial: The person resists the idea that he is going to die (e.g., he may reject or question his diagnosis or prognosis).

Stage 2 – Anger: The person expresses anger toward family, healthy people, caregivers, God, etc.

Stage 3 – Bargaining: This stage emerges when the person begins to recognize that his death may be coming; he bargains in an effort to attain a reprieve from death (e.g., he asks God or another higher power to allow him to live long enough to complete a particular activity or attend a specific event).

Stage 4 – Depression: Depression may occur when the person loses hope that he will recover.

Stage 5 – Acceptance: Acceptance is achieved when the person accepts that death is coming and has worked through the earlier stages and his fear of death.

These stages may overlap and do not always occur in sequence. Additionally, many individuals move back and forth among these stages, and some get stuck in one stage.

K. Moral Development

Moral development is defined as the ability to distinguish right from wrong and to then act in accordance with that distinction.

1. Piaget's Theory of Moral Development: Piaget studied moral development by questioning children about dilemmas related to the violation of game rules. He concluded that children progress through three stages of moral development:

Premoral stage (before age 6): Children in this stage exhibit little (if any) concern for rules.

Heteronomous morality (or "morality of constraint"; ages 7 through 10): During this stage, children believe that rules are set by authority figures and are unalterable. When judging whether an act is "right" or "wrong," they consider whether a rule has been violated and what the consequences of the act are – the greater the negative consequences, the worse the act.

Autonomous morality (or "morality of cooperation"; begins at age 11): Children in this stage view rules as being arbitrary and alterable when the people who are governed by them agree to change them. When judging an act, they focus more on the intention of the actor than on the act's consequences.

2. Children's Conceptions About Lying: Piaget also explored children's conceptions about lying. He concluded that very young children are "spontaneous liars" and consider their false statements to be "natural" and harmless. By age 7 or 8, children begin to intentionally communicate false statements; by age 10 or 11, they recognize that they can be deceived by others.

Subsequent research has suggested that children as young as age 3 or 4 lie intentionally, most often to avoid punishment or obtain a reward (Ceci et al., 1992). Children at this age may lie for other reasons, as well, such as to keep a promise, avoid embarrassment, and achieve personal gain.

3. Kohlberg's Theory of Moral Development: Kohlberg developed what he considered to be a universal, invariant sequence of three levels of moral development – preconventional,

conventional, and postconventional – that are each subdivided into two stages. Kohlberg (1971) further proposed that progression through these stages depends not only on level of reasoning but also on the individual's motivation (needs), opportunities to take on the perspective of others, and exposure to social institutions that foster equality and reciprocity (i.e., democratic institutions).

Level 1: Preconventional morality

Punishment and obedience orientation: The goodness and badness of an act depends on its consequences. For children at this stage, the right course of action is the one that allows them to avoid punishment.

Instrumental hedonism: Consequences still guide moral judgments, but judgments are based more on obtaining rewards and satisfying personal needs than on avoiding punishment.

Level 2: Conventional morality

"Good boy/good girl" orientation: The right action is the one that is liked or approved of by others.

Law and order orientation: In this stage, moral judgments are based on the rules and laws established by legitimate authorities.

Level 3: Postconventional morality

Morality of contract, individual rights, and democratically accepted laws: The morally right action is the one that is consistent with democratically determined laws (which can be changed if they interfere with basic rights).

Morality of individual principles of conscience: Right and wrong are determined on the basis of broad, self-chosen universally applicable ethical principles.

Although there are individual differences, people typically shift from the preconventional to the conventional level at about age 10 or 11, and from the conventional to the postconventional level in late adolescence or adulthood.

L. Social Growth and Development

1. Social Regulation, Social Role Taking, and Sociability:

a. Social Regulation: Children gradually internalize self-control of their behavior, emotions, and cognitions during the course of early and middle childhood. Parent behaviors that help a child internalize self-control and learn cooperation include acknowledging the child's feelings and teaching him to use alternative behaviors and ways of expressing his feelings (e.g., assertive rather than aggressive behavior). By contrast, children who are simply taught that they have to obey social rules tend to act out in the absence of a threat of punishment.

b. Social Role Taking: Social role-taking ability (i.e., the reduction of egocentric thought) is necessary for the emergence of prosocial behaviors. Before about age 6, children do not have the cognitive ability to see things from other people's perspectives. This skill develops gradually during childhood as a result of social role-taking opportunities in which children are exposed to perspectives that differ from their own.

Despite their renewed egocentrism, most adolescents are capable of recognizing and taking into account a consensual group perspective (one reflected in a social system and its laws, values, morals, etc.). Additionally, by about age 12, children can accurately infer other people's feelings, thoughts, and intentions. Although younger children have some ability to make these inferences, they often base their conclusions on physical observations that may not be correct (e.g., they don't realize that people may conceal their true feelings).

c. Sociability: Longitudinal studies suggest that sociability is a very stable trait and that, by age 2, children's social behaviors, such as initiation of social interactions and time spent interacting with other children, are fairly predictable (Cillessen et al., 2000). Children's social skills can be enhanced by their participation in preschool (Shea, 1981).

Baumrind (1971) examined factors in parent-child relationship that promote sociability and found that warm, supportive parents who set reasonable expectations for their children's social interactions tend to raise socially competent children; and that permissive parents who do not set or enforce social rules tend to raise children who are more aggressive, rebellious, and uncooperative. Unsociable children may have difficulties in middle childhood and adolescence, when peer rejection can produce or intensify emotional and behavioral problems.

2. Children's Play: Play is an important contributor to a child's physical, cognitive, social, and emotional development. Motor play, for example, assists in the development of children's muscles and motor coordination; rough-and-tumble play teaches children how to express impulses and feelings in socially acceptable ways; and pretend play (imaginative, make-believe, or symbolic play) provides opportunities to develop cognitive abilities related to symbolizing, imitation, and problem-solving and to practice behaviors in a situation that requires less accuracy than would be required in reality. Children engaged in **pretend play** may use their environment or objects within it as symbolic of something else (e.g., a cardboard box becomes a TV). Pretend play begins between 9 and 30 months of age and peaks at about age 4 or 5.

a. Functional and Constructive Play: At the beginning of the preschool years, children engage in functional play, which consists of simple repetitive activities. Functional play is primarily a way of being active, rather than a means of creating or building something. Beginning at about age 4, children begin to engage in constructive play, in which they manipulate objects to build or create something. This form of play allows children to practice their fine motor skills, test their developing physical and cognitive abilities, and learn to cooperate with others.

b. Social Aspects of Preschool Play: In **solitary play**, a child plays alone – he is engaged in a task, but not with other children. This form of play is typical of 2 to 3 year olds. Although solitary play is often viewed as immature, studies have shown that it often involves educational and goal-directed activities that contribute to a child's development. **Social play** takes several forms that emerge in an overlapping, stage-like way:

- **Parallel play** occurs when children play with similar toys and do similar things, but do not interact with each other. This form of play is common during the early preschool years.

- **Onlooker play** occurs when children watch others play, but do not participate themselves. Some children watch silently and others make comments, such as giving advice or encouragement.

- **Associative play** involves two or more children interacting with one another by sharing or borrowing toys or material; the children, however, are engaged in separate activities.
- **Cooperative play** involves children actually playing with one another, taking turns, playing games, making rules, etc.

Associative and cooperative play are more sophisticated forms of social play that usually do not emerge until the end of the preschool years. Children with substantial preschool experience, however, may engage in more sophisticated forms of social play earlier in the preschool years than children with less preschool or other social experience (Roopnarine et al., 1994). Additionally, solitary and onlooker play generally continue even among children who also engage in more sophisticated forms of play (e.g., sometimes an older preschool child will be in the mood to play by himself, or a child entering a new group may use onlooker play as a strategy for eventually joining the group).

c. Imaginary Friends: Preschool children, especially those without siblings, sometimes invent an imaginary friend. Imaginary friends can serve a variety of purposes, including allowing the child to experiment with new (sometimes negative or scary) behaviors and feelings, providing companionship, and fostering creativity. Having an imaginary friend during the preschool years is considered normal and is only rarely a symptom of psychopathology.

3. Peer and Social Relationships: The nature of peer and other relationships vary over the lifespan and depend on several factors including the individual's age and gender.

a. Friendships in Childhood and Adolescence: Damon (1988) has described differences in friendships during childhood and adolescence in terms of three developmental stages:

- The first stage occurs between the ages of 4 and 7. In this stage, friends are "playmates" (children who like each other and enjoy playing together).
- From ages 8 through 10, trust and assistance are critical aspects of friendship, and children believe that friends are a source of help and support.
- Beginning at about age 11, intimacy and loyalty become important factors. For preadolescents and adolescents, friends do not "deceive, reject, or abandon you."

Gender differences in friendship become apparent during the school years: Females are drawn more to the emotional and intimate aspects of friendships, and they have more exclusive friendships and engage in more intimate self-disclosure than males. In contrast, males place greater emphasis on shared interests and activities, have a larger number of friends, and spend more time participating in large groups (Clark & Bittle, 1992; Erwin, 1993).

b. Peer Status: Children who are popular with their peers have good social and communication skills and regularly engage in prosocial behaviors (i.e., they often empathize, share, and cooperate with others). They also tend to be self-confident, happy, and enthusiastic, and they are able to control their negative emotions (e.g., Rubin, Bukowski, & Parker, 1998).

At the other extreme are rejected and neglected children. *Rejected-aggressive children* tend to be hostile, hyperactive, and impulsive and have difficulty regulating negative emotions and taking the perspective of others. In contrast, *rejected-withdrawn children* have a high degree of social anxiety, tend to be submissive, have negative expectations about how others will treat them, and are often the victims of bullies (Berk, 2004). Finally, *neglected children* have fewer-than-average interactions with peers and rarely engage in disruptive behaviors. For many of these children, being alone is desirable, and they do not report being particularly lonely or unhappy (Berk, 2004; McDevitt & Ormrod, 2007). The research on rejected and neglected children has found that, overall, outcomes are worse for children who are actively rejected by their peers: Rejected children not only express greater loneliness and peer dissatisfaction but are also less likely to experience an improvement in peer status when they change social groups (e.g., Coie & Kupersmidt, 1983).

c. Bullying: Bullying tends to have short-term and long-term consequences for both victims and perpetrators. Children who are persistently bullied tend to have poorer grades and higher rates of truancy and dropping out and may experience a loss of self-esteem and feelings of isolation that can last into adulthood (Dupper, 2003). Children who bully have a much higher risk of ending up in juvenile court, being convicted of crimes in early adulthood, and themselves having children with aggression problems.

d. Peer Influence and Peer Pressure in Adolescence: Although peer influence during adolescence is generally stronger for prosocial behaviors than antisocial ones, at about age 14 or 15, peer conformity peaks, and it is at this time that adolescents are most responsive to *all* types of peer influence – neutral, positive, and negative (e.g., Leventhal, 1994). Compliance to peer pressure generally declines in later adolescence with a few important exceptions: Older adolescents report the greatest degree of peer pressure related to smoking, drinking alcohol, and engaging in sexual intercourse (Brown, Clasen, & Eicher, 1986).

Finally, studies comparing the relative influence of peers and parents during adolescence have found that peers have more influence than parents with regard to everyday issues such as music, clothing, and social activities. In contrast, parents are more influential when it comes to basic beliefs and values and educational and career goals (Sebald, 1986).

e. Gangs: For adolescents, gang membership can help fulfill their developmental need to associate with and be accepted by a peer group. The gang may also provide social support and protection from rival gangs.

The primary risk factor for gang membership is growing up in a neighborhood with poverty where there is low attachment to people and social institutions (Huff, 2001). Parent-related risk factors include absent parents, a lack of supervision, and parental substance abuse. School-related risk factors include low attachment to school and low expectations on the part of the student, parents, and teachers for success in school. Additionally, peers often have a significant impact on a young person's decision to join a gang.

f. Peer Relationships in Adulthood: In adulthood, the quality of peer relationships seems to be more important than the quantity. Having at least one confidant, for instance, helps ensure emotional well-being. In addition, research on the **buffering hypothesis** shows that the subjective perception of social support is more critical than actual support, not only for alleviating feelings of loneliness but also for reducing the effects of stress and the risk for coronary heart disease (Seeman, 1985; Ward, Sherman, & LaGory, 1984).

In late adulthood, friends can be important sources of emotional support and shared experiences. Older adults tend to socialize less often than younger adults, however, and many prefer to spend time with just a few close friends and family members who provide comfortable and reliable interactions. Older individuals who live alone or lack family ties are at high risk for social isolation unless they build a support network of friends and neighbors and/or are connected to formal resources in their communities.

4. Prosocial Behavior: "Prosocial behaviors" are actions that are performed with the intention of helping another person.

a. Empathy in Children: Empathy, or "the ability to recognize and respond sympathetically to the feelings of others" (Berk, 1998, p. 250), consists of two components – cognitive and affective – and is believed to be the result of language and cognitive development as well as early experiences, especially experiences with caregivers. With regard to the latter, parents who are responsive, nonpunitive, and nonauthoritarian, who model empathetic behavior, and who reason with children about the consequences of their behavior have children with the highest levels of empathy (e.g., Eisenberg-Berg & Mussen, 1978; Radke-Yarrow & Zahn-Waxler, 1984).

b. Sharing in Childhood: Children generally share by age 3, when they do so because sharing makes play more fun. By age 4, children begin to show more empathic sharing as they start to recognize other people's feelings and internalize the belief that they have an obligation to share (Eisenberg, 1982). Most children at this age do not fully understand the concept of sharing as a form of altruism, however, and, often, they share simply because it helps them get what they want. Adults usually encourage children to share, but peers influence sharing even more by providing opportunities to share and reinforcement for doing so through their responses (Grusec et al., 2002). In addition, children who observe others sharing are more likely to share.

5. Aggression: Children begin expressing aggressiveness early in life; and, by the preschool years, two types of aggressive behavior can be distinguished: Instrumental aggression is used to achieve an objective (e.g., to obtain an object); while hostile aggression is used to harm another person (Berk, 2004).

a. Theories of Aggression:

Frustration-aggression hypothesis: One version of this hypothesis claims that frustration creates a readiness for aggression (anger arousal), but that the actual expression of aggression requires both anger arousal and the presence of appropriate external (aggressive) cues (Berkowitz, 1971).

Social learning theory: Bandura's (1983) social learning theory describes aggressive behavior as the result of observational learning (imitation). Bandura had children observe a model act aggressively toward an inflatable "Bobo" doll. When children were subsequently left alone with the doll, they displayed aggressive behaviors similar to those of the model. These studies showed that a child is more likely to imitate an aggressive model when the model is powerful, successful, liked, and/or familiar; is of the same sex as the child; and is rewarded for acting aggressively.

b. Factors Associated With Aggression in Children:

Family factors: Patterson and his colleagues (1992) focus on family contributions to aggression and conclude that the families of highly aggressive boys are distinguishable from other families in terms of two main characteristics: coercive interactions (reliance on coercive, aggressive behaviors by both children and their parents to gain compliance) and poor parental monitoring of children's activities. Their **coercive family interaction model** proposes (a) that children initially learn aggressive behaviors from their parents who rarely reinforce prosocial behaviors, use harsh discipline, and reward their children's aggressiveness with approval and attention, and (b) that, over time, aggressive parent-child interactions escalate. These investigators also contend that the likelihood that parents will use coercive forms of discipline increases when the family experiences high levels of stress, the parents have certain personality characteristics, and the child has a difficult temperament. Patterson et al. developed a parent intervention that is designed to stop this coercive cycle by teaching parents effective child management skills and providing them with therapy to help them cope more effectively with stress (Patterson, Chamberlain, & Reid, 1982).

Social-cognitive factors: Researchers have also identified several **social-cognitive factors** that contribute to aggression. Perry and colleagues (Perry & Busey, 1977; Perry, Perry, & Rasmussen, 1986) found that aggressive children differ from their less aggressive peers in terms of (a) self-efficacy beliefs (they are more likely to say that it is easy to perform aggressive acts but difficult to inhibit aggressive impulses); (b) beliefs about the outcomes of their behaviors (they expect that aggression will be followed by positive consequences including reduced aversive treatment by others); and (c) regret or remorse (they show little remorse after committing an aggressive act). Other studies have linked aggression to a tendency to misinterpret the positive or ambiguous acts of others as intentionally hostile (Dodge et al., 1990).

c. Gender and Aggression: Aggressiveness has been consistently linked to gender, with the studies finding that boys are more aggressive than females in a variety of contexts: For example, boys engage in more "rough-and-tumble" play, exhibit greater physical aggression, and are more dominant with peers. Gender differences in aggressiveness seem to be due to both biological and environmental factors and are greatest among preschoolers and then gradually decline with increasing age up through the college years. Note that recent research suggests that the usual generalization about gender differences in aggression needs to be qualified: While boys are more overtly (verbally and physically) aggressive than girls, girls show more relational aggression, which means that they attempt to harm or exert control over others by withdrawing their friendship and acceptance (Crick & Grotpeter, 1995).

d. Reducing Aggression: Methods that have been found useful for reducing childhood aggression include modeling and reinforcing alternative prosocial behaviors. One technique that seems particularly effective is **cognitive training**, which Zahavi and Asher (1978) successfully used with highly aggressive preschool boys. Their intervention included teaching boys that (a) aggression hurts other people and causes unhappiness; (b) aggression doesn't solve problems; and (c) conflicts can be successfully resolved in other ways. The effectiveness of this intervention is consistent with research showing that empathy is an important motivator for moral behavior (Hoffman, 1987) and that inductive disciplinary techniques foster the development of empathy (Eisenberg, 1992).

M. Sexual Growth and Development

1. Sexual Behavior in Children: Children as young as preschool age explore their own "private parts" or show them to others. Between the ages of 4 and 6, some children purposefully touch their own genitals (masturbate) or explore them with other children of the same age (e.g., "play doctor"). All of these behaviors are fairly common and considered a normal part of sexual development.

Generally sexual exploration and play by children is considered *typical* (i.e., not a sign of a problem) when it has the following characteristics: (a) the children involved in the play know each other well and play together often; (b) the play occurs between children who are of about the same age and size; (c) the play is infrequent; (d) the play is spontaneous; (e) the play is voluntary on the part of both children and neither child is uncomfortable or upset by it; and (f) the children are easily diverted from the behavior when told to stop. Conversely, sexual play by children is *atypical* and may signal a problem (e.g., perhaps that one of the children has been sexually abused) when (a) it includes behavior that is clearly beyond the child's developmental stage; (b) it involves threats, force, or aggression; (c) the children are of very different ages (e.g., a 4 year old and a 10 year old); and/or (d) it causes anxiety, anger, or other strong emotions in one or both of the children (NCTSN, 2009).

Parents who find their child engaged in sexual play are encouraged to speak calmly with the child about the behavior. Assuming that the child is not visibly upset by the play behavior, the parents should seek more information about what has happened by asking primarily open-ended questions that avoid leading the child. The parents should also use the event as an opportunity to talk with the child about healthy boundaries (e.g., the child has the right to say "no") and appropriate/inappropriate sexual behavior (e.g., "okay" and "not okay" touches).

2. Adolescent Sexuality: Due to prohibitions learned in the family, some adolescents develop strong feelings of guilt for engaging in sexual behavior that is common and normal, such as masturbation.

a. Gender Differences: Because girls generally enter puberty about two years earlier than boys, they may start dating and having sexual experiences at an earlier age. However, adolescent girls, on the whole, are less sexually active than boys of a comparable age. For girls, sexual impulses and activity are usually associated with other feelings, especially feelings of love. Boys are more likely to separate love and sexual desire.

b. Experimentation With Sexual Roles and Behaviors: During adolescence, experimentation with sexual behavior and different sexual roles is common. Some adolescents have homosexual experiences. In some instances, these teenagers are, indeed, gay and may require help in coming to terms with their sexual orientation. For other teens, these experiences are transient, and they may need reassurance that isolated homosexual behavior is normal.

Adolescents (as well as adults) may also experiment with **autoerotic asphyxia** (i.e., asphyxia caused by intentionally strangling or suffocating oneself while masturbating). This behavior is based on the individual's belief that reduced oxygen flow to the brain will enhance orgasm. A variety of physical props may be used when engaging in this activity, including a plastic bag, hanging platform, or a basin filled with water. The behavior associated with autoerotic asphyxia is not usually suicidal in intent, but it does pose a danger of accidental death.

c. Lesbian, Gay, Bisexual, and Transgendered (LGBT) Youth: LGBT youth may experience harassment or violence; are at risk of experiencing isolation, low self-esteem, depression, and substance abuse; may have a difficult time coping with their concerns about secrecy; and have a potential for suicide that is two to three times higher than that of other adolescents (Kaplan, 2004). LGBT youth of color are vulnerable to both racism and homophobia and must adapt to living in three different communities – their ethnic community, the gay and lesbian community, and the majority community.

3. Research by Masters and Johnson and Kaplan: Masters and Johnson (1970) estimated that about 50 percent of married couples in the U.S. have sexual problems. Assuming there is no physiological cause, these problems are most commonly due to ignorance about sexuality and resulting **performance anxiety**, a lack of open communication, and/or the effects of rigid sexual values. Masters and Johnson view the sexual response as a single entity, with four stages: excitement, plateau, orgasmic, and resolution.

Kaplan (1974, 1987) asserted that a female's inability to orgasm with coital stimulation alone may be a normal variant of the female sexual response (i.e., it is not necessarily a sexual dysfunction). Subsequent research has found that 70 percent of women surveyed required more than coital stimulation to reach orgasm. Kaplan describes a **tri-phasic model** of sexual response:

Desire phase: Sexual activity for both genders begins with an appetitive phase, produced by the activation of a specific neural system in the brain. Other research suggests that, although biological and hormonal factors evoking desire are very similar in the two genders, men and women differ in terms of the external stimuli that evoke interest in sex: Males are more "turned on" by visual and other sensory stimulation, while females respond more to a whole complex of "courting" behaviors.

Excitement phase: In both sexes, a vascular reflex causes the genital organs to become engorged with blood (i.e., erection of the penis, lubrication and ballooning of the vaginal canal). The complex hydraulic system required for erection is more complicated than the parallel process of female excitement; thus, males are more likely to suffer from dysfunctions of this phase than females are.

Orgasm phase: Male orgasm consists of two distinct phases: emission and ejaculation. Females do not ejaculate; their orgasm consists of regular rhythmic contractions of the swollen tissues of the vaginal area and the pelvic floor muscles. Under ordinary circumstances, the orgasm reflex, unlike the vascular reflex of excitement, is under the individual's voluntary control. Males show a **refractory period** after orgasm, whereas females generally can become aroused soon after orgasm, making multiple orgasms for females possible. (A "refractory period" is a period of time following orgasm when it is physiologically impossible to have additional orgasms.)

4. Effects of Illness, Injury, and Drugs on Sexual Functioning: Biochemical impairment of the sexual response can result in sexual dysfunction. Any debilitating or chronic physical illness will tend to lower libido; **diabetes**, for example, may lower libido and impair arousal in both males and females. Stress can also produce certain kinds of sexual dysfunction, including impotence.

For many (if not most) individuals with spinal cord injury, sexual appetite and interest remain relatively unaffected. Many men with spinal cord injury are able to have intercourse. The higher the level of the injury, the more likely a man will experience reflexive erections, while psychic erections are more common with lower (and incomplete) lesions. Ejaculation is less likely, however, especially for men with complete lesions. For women, spinal cord injuries seem to have less effect – many women with these injuries report continued sexual arousal and lubrication. For both men and women, however, the incidence of orgasm is not known.

Drugs used to treat hypertension may cause impotence by impairing neurovascular reflexes, and certain psychoactive drugs (i.e., **antidepressants**) may produce sexual dysfunction as a side-effect. Hormones and certain stimulants (amphetamines, cocaine) may enhance libido and sexual functioning. Alcohol may reduce inhibitions about sex, but impairs the physiological processes of excitement and orgasm.

5. Effects of Aging on Sexual Activity and Functioning: Although the overall frequency of sexual activity does decrease with increasing age, a large proportion of older people are sexually active. Also, older people often report that affection and physical closeness have become increasingly important to them.

a. Factors That Determine Level of Sexual Activity: Sexual activity in mid-life and earlier is a good predictor of sexual activity in late adulthood, especially for males (Berk, 2004).

Among older adults who experience declines in sexual activity, men and women both report health problems as a primary reason for a lack of sexual activity. The lack of a sexual partner is also a frequently cited reason, especially by women (e.g., Burgess, 2004; Landau et al., 2007).

b. Changes in Sexual Functioning: In women, physical changes brought on as a result of estrogen depletion following menopause (see below) can result in discomfort during sexual intercourse. Men experience a steady decline in testosterone as they grow older beginning at about age 50. Older men take longer to achieve an erection and may require more tactile stimulation to do so. They can maintain an erection for a longer period of time but ejaculate with less force, and the refractory period becomes longer.

6. Menopause: Menopause occurs when a woman has not experienced a menstrual cycle for one year and is a gradual process that can take up to 20 years. The majority of women reach menopause between 45 and 55 years of age. Women who are childless and women who smoke are more likely to reach menopause earlier (Avis et al., 2002).

a. Potential Effects of Falling Estrogen Levels:

During menopause: (a) Many women experience hot flashes (a rise and fall in skin temperature accompanied by sweating and sometimes heart palpitations, nausea, and anxiety). Hot flashes occurring at night cause night sweats, which can interfere with sleep. (b) Insomnia may occur as a result of hot flashes and/or reductions in REM sleep. (c) Irritability and deficits in short-term memory and concentration may occur, often as a result of sleep deprivation.

After menopause: (a) Effects of falling estrogen levels after menopause can include problems with bladder control; dry skin, thinning hair, and an increase in facial hair; vaginal dryness, reduced lubrication, and thinning of the vaginal walls and mucous membranes (which may result in pain during intercourse and susceptibility to infections); cardiovascular changes and rises in cholesterol and triglyceride levels (which increase the risk of heart disease); and an increase in bone loss (which places women at risk for osteoporosis). (b) Women who experience menopause before about age 50 are at greater risk for **osteoporosis** and heart disease than are women who reach menopause later (DeAngelis, 1997). Other factors associated with a higher risk of osteoporosis are white race, slender build, low calcium intake, smoking, and a lack of regular exercise. Physicians often recommend bone-density screening for women entering menopause.

b. Psychological Symptoms: Most women do not develop significant psychological symptoms as a result of the hormonal changes associated with menopause, but some women experience increased anger, anxiety, depression, or self-consciousness because of how they perceive the meaning of menopause. Women may also develop depression due to other changes associated with this phase of development (e.g., no longer feeling young, children leaving home). Culture also plays a role in a woman's feelings about menopause (e.g., in cultures in which a female's role is primarily to bear children, the inability to have any more children lowers a woman's status) (Adler et al., 2000).

c. Hormone Replacement Therapy: Hormone replacement therapy (HRT) is sometimes prescribed to treat the symptoms of menopause and help prevent the physical consequences of estrogen depletion. Concerns about HRT emerged, however, after studies revealed that women who took HRT had a slight increase in heart attacks, stroke, blood clots, breast cancer, and cognitive impairments (Rapp et al., 2003). The choice to take HRT should be left to the individual woman, based on the severity of her menopause symptoms, her risk of osteoporosis and heart disease, and, especially, her risk of developing breast cancer.

N. Spiritual Development

A client's spirituality encompasses not only their individual functioning, but their environmental system as well. Social workers should be competent in dealing with spiritual matters and guide their assessments to meet the needs and values of each client, focusing on health and wellness throughout the lifespan. Hodge (2004) expands the terminology of cultural competence to the more specific, spiritual competence. It can be described as characterized by the following: (a) an understanding of one's own spiritual values and worldview, and the associated assumptions, biases, and limitations; (b) an understanding of the client's spiritual worldview without any associated judgement; and (c) the ability to create and implement intervention techniques that match and are sensitive to the client's spiritual worldview (Ashford & Lecroy, 2013).

While spirituality and religion may not play a factor, it is important to understand that religious issues may also be central to the presenting problems brought to service. For example, an engaged couple may disagree about the role religion or spirituality may play in their wedding and overall future together. Thibault, Ellor, and Netting (1991) discuss three factors relevant to a client's spirituality: cognitive (the meaning given to specific events whether past or present), affective (a client's sense of connecting to a larger reality), and behavioral (how a client's beliefs are affirmed, such as worship or prayer). Thus, spirituality may affect the client's coping skills, sources, of support, etc. Social workers are encouraged to involve clergy or faith-based leaders when working conjointly in addressing personal and spiritual problems faced by clients (Hepworth et al., 2010).

III. Family Theories and Dynamics

A. Overview of "Family"

Hartman and Laird (1983, p. 576) state that a family develops when "two or more people construct an intimate environment that they define as a family, an environment in which they generally will share a living space, commitment, and a variety of the roles and functions usually considered part of family life." This definition encompasses not only families with a husband, wife, and children, but also single-parent families, gay or lesbian couples with or without children, extended family groupings, and other related or unrelated people who live together as a family group.

1. The Family as a Social System: The family is a social system. It is a whole comprised of interrelated parts, each part affects and is affected by the other parts, and each part contributes to the functioning of the whole. To understand a family system, it is necessary to consider its structure (subsystems, boundaries, etc.); goals, communication patterns, and development; as well as the external influences that affect it such as extended family members, friends, the neighborhood, the church or other religious body, the school system, the workplace, the community, public policy, etc. (For more information on assessing families, see Section IV of Assessment.)

2. The Family Life-Cycle: The family life-cycle is a longitudinal view of family development that suggests that a family passes through expected phases in much the same way as an individual develops through psychosocial stages. Stages of the family life-cycle are demarcated by entrances and exits of family members and the shifts in role function that these changes in membership require. Carter and McGoldrick (1980) describe six stages of the family life-cycle:

Stage 1 – between families (the unattached young adult).

Stage 2 – joining families through marriage (the newly married couple).

Stage 3 – the family with young children.

Stage 4 – the family with adolescents.

Stage 5 – launching children and moving on (a.k.a. the **empty nest**).

Stage 6 – the family in later life.

According to family life-cycle theories, symptoms in individual family members are an expression of the family's struggle to adapt to the demands of a new stage. Stage 3, when the first child appears, and Stage 5, when there are many entrances and exits, are seen as the most stressful stages. Traumatic experiences, such as early death, unemployment, or the birth of a child with a disability, may make it difficult for a family to achieve the necessary developmental tasks of each stage. A rigid and dysfunctional family structure also increases the chances that normal developmental change will be experienced as a crisis.

B. Marriage

1. Adjustment to Marriage: Challenges associated with adjusting to marriage include learning to communicate effectively, learning to deal with conflict, creating common goals, learning to derive satisfaction from the relationship, negotiating gender differences in how men and women perceive marriage, establishing new routines for daily living, and establishing a joint budget. Additionally, newly married couples, especially those who believe common myths about marriage, may need to adapt their expectations about what marriage is like. In working with couples planning to marry or adjusting to marriage, it may be important to begin by discussing **marital myths** and expectations: Marital problems often develop when one or both partners have unrealistic expectations, such as assuming that marital satisfaction will automatically increase over time.

2. Satisfaction and Conflict in Marriage:

a. Marital Satisfaction: Higher levels of marital satisfaction have been linked to several factors including partner similarity in age, socioeconomic status, education, and religion; marrying after age 23; dating for at least six months prior to marriage; and waiting to have children until at least one year after marriage (Berk, 2004). Several cross-sectional studies conducted in the 1960s and 1970s found a U-shaped relationship between marital duration and martial satisfaction, with the greatest dissatisfaction occurring during the middle years of marriage. Although these findings are frequently cited in textbooks, a number of subsequent studies using different methodologies have not supported this pattern but, instead, have found either no relationship, a negative relationship, or a positive relationship between marital duration and satisfaction. For example, VanLaningham, Johnson, and Amato's (2001) longitudinal study suggested that martial satisfaction either declines steadily over time or initially declines and then stabilizes.

Finally, according to Gottman (1994), a key to marital satisfaction is the balance between the couple's positive and negative emotional interactions – satisfied couples have many more positive than negative interactions.

b. Marital Conflict: Anger targeted at a specific issue or behavior and expressed to one's partner in a respectful way can promote marital satisfaction. In contrast, marital difficulties are likely to arise when expressions of anger include criticism, contempt, defensiveness, or stonewalling and are directed at the partner rather than at the partner's behaviors (Gottman, 1994).

In addition, marital conflicts sometimes escalate because men and women have different approaches to conflict: Women tend to pursue a conflict with emotion, while men tend to avoid a conflict through rationalizations, the "silent treatment," and physical withdrawal.

3. Marital Relationships at Midlife:

a. Distancing Due to Differing Goals: People at midlife may begin to pursue new goals for themselves. For instance, a woman may refocus on her career, while a man may begin to place more emphasis on "family time." For some midlife couples, a sense of distance develops because the husband and wife are working toward different goals. Wallerstein (1995) has suggested that a midlife couple's ability to handle this change depends on each spouse's level of commitment to the relationship and ability to understand and accept his or her partner's needs.

b. Adjustments After Launching Children: Some couples at midlife are "launching" their adolescent children into adulthood, which can provide an opportunity to strengthen the marital bond. For some couples, however, marital tensions that were masked while they were raising children come to the surface after the children leave home. For instance, couples who experience **role overload** while raising their children may neglect their roles as spouses in favor of their roles as parents. Over time this can lead to a loss of companionship and communication for the couple, resulting in reduced marital satisfaction and a need to reassess and rebuild their relationship once the children are gone. Couples also need to come to terms with their children's independence so that they can begin to develop adult-to-adult relationships with them.

4. Marital Relationships in Late Adulthood: Marital satisfaction is a strong predictor of life satisfaction and quality of life for older people who are married. Problems arising for married couples in late adulthood often center on impairment or illness of one of the spouses. Feelings of isolation, frustration, or even hostility may emerge if a spouse develops a sensory or cognitive impairment that requires significant changes in the couple's way of life or usual communication patterns (McInnes-Dittrich, 2005). Similarly, if one of the spouses develops a debilitating medical condition or dementia, the healthy spouse will often serve as his or her primary caregiver. Although spouses usually derive satisfaction from helping their partners, caregiving can be physically and emotionally draining, especially if the care required is intensive or long-term.

5. Widowhood: Adjustment to widowhood is more difficult when the marriage was very warm and intimate, the widowed spouse depended heavily on his or her partner for instrumental help (e.g., help with chores and other day-to-day activities), and/or the widowed spouse lacks adequate social support (Ashford et al., 2006). Widows and widowers who have difficulty adjusting to their loss are susceptible to depression. On the other hand, for older women who are relatively healthy and have adequate finances, widowhood can represent an opportunity for personal growth as they start to rely on their own resources for the first time, and they may not want to remarry. Older widowers, by contrast, are more likely to report wanting to find a new partner (Davidson, 2001).

C. Parenthood and Parenting

1. Transition to Parenthood: A couple's ability to adapt to parenthood is heavily influenced by the availability of social support (family, friends, neighbors, community programs, etc.). New mothers also fare better when they have a supportive relationship with their spouse or partner and when he assists her in caring for the baby and with household tasks. Additionally, once the baby is born, the parents must give up the "fantasy baby" they have dreamed about during the pregnancy and accept the baby that has been born.

New parents typically face the following challenges (Ashford et al., 2006): (a) adapting to the role of "parent" (e.g., deciding what kind of parent they want to be and identifying for themselves what makes a good parent); (b) adapting to changes in their priorities; (c) deciding how they will divide the new household tasks; (d) finding the time and energy required to keep their own relationship satisfying in terms of intimacy and companionship; (e) adapting to reduced amounts of free time (for many new parents, this change is the most difficult one to adapt to); and (f) handling an increase in stress.

The increase in stress can be especially challenging for the mother who may be exhausted after the birth process, is dealing with postpartum physical changes, and could be facing changes in her worklife. New mothers are particularly vulnerable to distress when they are the infant's primary caregiver and when they have a baby with a difficult temperament.

2. Factors That May Affect Parenting of a Newborn: Factors that may interfere with the ability of parents to provide an adequate environment for their newborn or respond to his needs include the mother's health status, postpartum depression, drug or alcohol addiction, mental illness, marital difficulties, developmental delays in the child, poverty, and adolescent parenthood. A few of these factors are described below; others are discussed elsewhere in this chapter.

Cesarean section: Caring for an infant while also recovering from surgery can be exhausting, and a mother's fatigue can interfere with her ability to interact appropriately with her infant. Additionally, some studies show that women who give birth by cesarean section are more likely to experience depression after giving birth.

Postpartum depression: Women with **postpartum depression** (PPD) tend to be less responsive to their infants and may have difficulty bonding with them. (a) *Early-onset PPD* ("baby blues") begins right after delivery, lasts for 10 to 12 days (without intervention), and is relatively mild. Its symptoms include sadness, tearfulness, anxiety, and difficulty sleeping. Typically the only treatment the new mother needs is reassurance and help with household chores and care of the baby. (b) *Later-onset PPD* is a more serious condition that usually becomes apparent several weeks after delivery. Its symptoms include severe mood swings; a lack of joy; intense irritability and anger; withdrawal from family and friends; feelings of shame, guilt, or inadequacy; loss of appetite; insomnia; overwhelming fatigue; loss of interest in sex; and thoughts of harming oneself or one's baby. Women who experience persistent depression after giving birth should discuss treatment alternatives with their doctor. Treatment can include counseling for the woman and her partner (for emotional support, assistance with problem-solving, etc.), antidepressant medication (this may be added to counseling when PPD is moderate or severe), parent coaching, and/or in-home assistance with care of the baby. (c) Finally, the most severe form of PPD is *postpartum psychosis*, in which the new mother experiences hallucinations or delusions about herself or her baby. Postpartum psychosis is a medical emergency that requires immediate attention. (Note: When using the DSM-5, the specifier "with peripartum onset" is applied to major depressive disorder, bipolar I disorder, and bipolar II disorder when the onset of symptoms is during pregnancy or within four weeks postpartum.)

Prenatal exposure to drugs: Because their nervous systems are disorganized and fragile, newborns who were exposed prenatally to drugs may be easily overwhelmed by sensory stimulation. In response to stimulation (including the sight of their parents), they tend to either cry or go to sleep, and this may make the parents feel rejected or inadequate. Additionally, parents who abuse drugs may not provide adequate nutrition, appropriate medical care, or a stimulating learning environment for their infant, and are at greater risk for abusing or neglecting their baby. Early intervention can allow children exposed to drugs to develop in a normal or near normal way.

Premature baby: Parents may hesitate to interact with their premature newborn because he appears fragile and is connected to medical equipment. Moreover, the infant's immature nervous system may cause him to be irritable, difficult to comfort, and easily overstimulated, and he may withdraw when his parents try to interact with him.

3. Parenting a Preschooler: Ideally, the parents of a preschooler will begin to foster independence in their child, allow him to try new activities, and teach him to follow rules and engage in acceptable social behavior by using such strategies as language, reason, and the setting of reasonable limits. Parents who impose unrealistic expectations on their preschooler or who are overly strict or demanding may cause the child to feel inadequate and/or guilty for failing to accomplish something on his own.

4. Parenting an Adolescent: Most parents and their adolescent children get along, and teenagers are generally receptive to guidance, approval, and correction from their parents. In most families, however, the transition to adolescence involves some stress for the adolescent and parents, and this may result in difficulties in the parent-child relationship. It's also worth noting that, along with adapting to changes in their adolescent child, many parents of teenagers are middle-aged and in the process of making changes in their own lives. Having a satisfying career and outside activities can help middle-aged parents cope better with parenting an adolescent (Steinberg, 1995).

a. Development of the Adolescent's Autonomy: Many parent-adolescent relational problems stem from the adolescent's emerging need to achieve independence from home and family. Ideally the parents of an adolescent are able to find an appropriate balance between letting go of full responsibility for him and still retaining a necessary amount of control. Many parents, however, have difficulty adapting to their adolescent's need for independence – some have trouble letting go at all or want to retain full control, some are unable to set appropriate limits, some lack the skills needed to grant independence, and some act out their unconscious or covert wishes through the lives of their adolescent child. An adolescent is most likely to develop a healthy sense of **autonomy** if his parents give him more decision-making authority than he had before. In a democratic family structure, for example, the parents retain final decision-making authority, but allow their adolescent to participate equally with them when decisions are being made.

b. Parent-Adolescent Conflict: Conflicts between an adolescent and his parents are common and usually begin when the child first enters adolescence. At that time, there is usually an increase in bickering and negative interactions and a decrease in expressions of affection and shared activities. Throughout the adolescent period, parent-child conflicts tend to center on mundane, everyday issues such as chores, curfew, and homework.

Many parent-child conflicts during this period stem from the adolescent's tendency to resist or rebel against authority or control. When adolescents acquire the capacity for social reasoning, for example, they often begin to view certain rules as arbitrary social conventions that they should not be required to follow (Smetana, 2000). When this happens, an adolescent and his parents may begin to perceive family rules in dissimilar ways. For example, parents may require their adolescent to keep his room clean (a social convention), but the adolescent may perceive the subject of a clean room to be a matter of personal choice.

5. Parental Disciplinary Strategies: Hoffman (1970) has identified three parental disciplinary strategies:

Power-assertive discipline (punishment): This strategy emphasizes physical punishment, threat of punishment, and physical efforts to control a child's behavior. Research shows that using this form of discipline tends to increase children's aggressive tendencies, perhaps because the parents are modeling aggressive behavior and teaching that conflict is best resolved through fighting and threats of harm. Moreover, children who feel ashamed and embarrassed when physically punished by their parents may develop low self-esteem, which makes them more likely to respond to others in an aggressive way, often because they lack appropriate social skills.

Love withdrawal: This strategy involves withdrawing love when a child's behavior is considered inappropriate (e.g., ignoring the child, giving him the "silent treatment," verbally discounting him, threatening to send him away, suggesting that he isn't loved anymore because of his behavior). Children of parents who use this strategy tend to be excessively anxious and to have difficulty expressing their emotions.

Induction: **Induction** involves using explanation and rationality to influence a child's behaviors. Using this disciplinary strategy provides children with opportunities to learn how to exercise self-control and helps them develop internal moral standards. Compared to children who are punished, these children tend to be more thoughtful and generous toward others (Turiel, 2000).

6. Gay and Lesbian Parents: Studies evaluating the effects of having a gay or lesbian parent on a child's development suggest that the nature of the parent-child relationship is more important than a parent's sexual orientation: Overall, children of gay and lesbian parents are similar to children of heterosexual parents in terms of social relations, psychological adjustment, cognitive functioning, gender identity development, gender role behavior, and sexual orientation (e.g., Anderssen, Amlie, & Ytteroy, 2002; Brewaeys et al., 1997; Tasker, 2005). In addition, the studies have confirmed that the parenting skills of lesbian mothers and gay fathers are similar (or even superior) to those of matched heterosexual couples. For example, Flaks et al. (1995) found that the parenting awareness skills of lesbian couples were stronger than those of heterosexual couples. There is also evidence that the childrearing problems encountered by lesbian and heterosexual single mothers are similar and that children being raised by a single lesbian or single heterosexual mother do not differ significantly in terms of socio-emotional development (e.g., MacCallum & Golombok, 2008).

7. Other Parent Factors Affecting Parenting:

a. Parents With Mental Illness: Children of parents with mental illness have a higher-than-average risk for emotional and behavioral problems and for developing mental illness themselves because of both genetic factors and their parents' behaviors: When left untreated, conditions such as bipolar disorder, schizophrenia, chronic depression, and alcohol or drug addiction usually interfere with parent-child interactions and can jeopardize a child's safety. When working with parents who have serious mental disorders or intellectual disability (see below), it's important to balance the rights of the parents and those of their children – achieving this balance can be difficult when children are at risk of receiving inadequate or dangerous care.

b. Parents With Intellectual Disability: Although mothers and fathers with intellectual disability may lack some of the skills required for effective and safe parenting, federal and state laws guarantee equality to people with disabilities, including the right to have and raise children. These parents can often benefit from in-home assistance and parenting programs, and they tend to fare better when there is another adult in the home (Bromwich, 1985). In particular, mothers with intellectual disability frequently live with their own parents, who provide daily support and help with child care.

c. Parents' Income and Educational Status: Lower-income parents and less educated parents tend be to more authoritarian with their children – they may expect more obedience from them, engage in less verbal interaction, and display less warmth (Maccoby, 1980). A number of explanations have been offered to account for this, including the following: (a) these parents face greater stress in their lives; (b) lower-income mothers may not receive adequate prenatal care and, as a result, give birth to premature, low-birth-weight, or drug-exposed babies who tend to be more difficult to care for; and (c) lower-socioeconomic status parents may believe that authoritarian parenting is necessary to protect their children from drug use, delinquency, school dropout, early pregnancy, and other risks (Shaffer, 2002). There is evidence that low-income parents in inner cities who establish and enforce strict rules for their children, while also providing ample warmth, may help their children withstand negative environmental influences that place them at risk for delinquency and low school achievement (McLoyd, 1998).

8. Adolescent Pregnancy and Parenthood: A teenage expectant mother may not get adequate prenatal care during the first three months of her pregnancy, resulting in an increased risk of low birth-weight and infant mortality.

Adolescent parents tend to be less responsive to the infant and to engage in less verbal interaction with him (which can interfere with the development of attachment); may fail to provide the infant with sufficient cognitive stimulation; and are themselves at risk of developmental problems (i.e., they may have problems developing their own identity while caring for an infant). Additionally, many adolescent parents lack adequate knowledge about developmental milestones and child development – they may have unrealistically high developmental expectations for their baby or fail to recognize developmental problems. Finally, adolescent parents are more likely than adult parents to perceive their infants as "difficult" and to use punitive disciplinary strategies. With toddlers, adolescent parents tend to be less sensitive, more intrusive, and more negative in their interactions.

Factors contributing to "successful" adolescent motherhood include the adolescent mother having a realistic view of her situation, taking charge of her life and using available community resources, and having supportive relationships that she can rely on, including with her parents and the baby's father (Ashford et al., 2006). Other factors useful for helping adolescents succeed as mothers (and fathers) include being able to complete their education and receiving assistance to cope with depression, increase their self-esteem, and understand their baby's temperament (Osofsky et al., 1993).

If feasible, the adolescent father should be included when decisions are being made about a teenage pregnancy and caring for the child after birth. Support for the father should continue beyond the first year of the baby's life, if possible, because his involvement in the child's life is more likely to diminish over time if he feels overwhelmed by the demands of raising a child or providing financial support.

D. Grandparenthood

1. Benefits of Grandparenthood: Grandparenting can play a significant role in facilitating adaptation to the aging process – it provides a new role for older people at a time when they are losing other roles and allows them to have an influence on future generations of their family, which can help them come to terms with their own lives and with death.

2. Grandparents Raising Grandchildren: Grandparents sometimes take over responsibility for raising their grandchildren. This tends to occur when circumstances such as substance abuse, physical or mental illness, incarceration, poverty, or homelessness render the grandchildren's parents unable to care for them. These grandparents usually face a number of stressors beyond those associated with taking on renewed parenting duties. For example, they may (a) become isolated from peers who are no longer raising children, (b) be required to provide special care if their grandchildren have emotional or behavioral problems associated with having been abused or neglected, (c) worry about becoming sick and unable to care for their grandchildren, and/or (d) be deeply concerned about their own children's well-being (Ashford et al., 2006).

Additionally, some of these grandparents are living on fixed incomes, unemployed, or working at low-paying jobs and need to rely on public social agencies to provide resources and services for their grandchildren. Formal support systems for grandparents raising grandchildren are available through such organizations as the American Association of Retired Persons (AARP), and, in some communities, kinship care centers are available. These centers offer counseling, support groups, parent-skills training, and advice on obtaining guardianship.

E. Divorce

1. Predictors of Divorce: A number of demographic characteristics have been identified as predictors of divorce. For example, results of the National Survey of Family Growth (National Center for Health Statistics, 2002) indicate that, for women, the risk for divorce is greatest when they marry at a young age, have a lower level of education, have no religious affiliation, are in a mixed-ethnic relationship, come from a single-parent home, were raped, had a child prior to marriage or within seven months of marriage, or cohabited with their partner before marriage.

Risk for divorce has also been linked to the married couple's interactional style. A 14-year longitudinal study by Gottman and Levenson (2000) identified two interaction patterns that are predictive of divorce: (a) The *emotionally volatile attack-defend pattern* is predictive of earlier divorce and is characterized by escalating negativity. This pattern is consistent with previous research by Gottman and colleagues (e.g., Gottman, 1994), which revealed that it is how anger is dealt with (rather than the anger itself) that accurately predicts the risk for divorce. We touched on this research earlier in this section. Specifically, these investigators found that the expression of anger is predictive of marital dissatisfaction and divorce when it consistently involves a combination of criticism, contempt, defensiveness, and stonewalling (the "Four Horsemen of the Apocalypse"). (b) The *emotionally inexpressive pattern* is predictive of later divorce and is characterized by suppression of both positive and negative affect. Couples exhibiting this pattern not only avoid conflict but also self-disclosure and any other form of emotional engagement.

2. Effects of Divorce on Men and Women: Although divorce ultimately has benefits for unhappy couples (e.g., increased sense of control over one's life, less day-to-day unhappiness), both men and women experience high levels of stress as a result of divorce and may continue to feel overwhelmed for at least a year. Anger and sadness are common. Women who have physical custody of the children may feel overwhelmed by their responsibilities; men may become depressed about having less contact with their children; the former partners may have difficulty finding new ways of relating to each other; and both men and women may struggle to redefine themselves as single people, feel isolated, and feel a loss of self-confidence as they begin to try out new relationships. The stressors associated with divorce also place individuals at higher risk for depression, substance abuse, and physical health problems (Amato, 2000). Adjustment to divorce is usually more difficult for the partner who did not initiate the divorce, for individuals with little income, and for individuals who do not develop new supportive relationships in their lives. Regarding income, the consequences of divorce tend to be more severe for women who did not work outside the home during the marriage, including those who wanted or were able to stay home to care for their children. These women may have depended on marriage for financial security and they might have few options for securing an adequate and reliable income following divorce.

3. Effects of Divorce on Parenting: Following divorce, parents experience emotional distress and changes in functioning that often include a "**diminished capacity to parent**" (Wallerstein & Blakeslee, 1990): The mother, who usually has physical custody of the children, is frequently socially isolated and lonely and experiences a decline in income. She tends to be uncommunicative, impatient, and less warm and loving toward her children (especially sons), and she monitors her children's activities less closely and is less consistent but more authoritarian in terms of punishment. Custodial fathers have similar problems, although they may adjust to their situation sooner than custodial mothers (Hetherington & Stanley-Hagan, 1986). Noncustodial fathers are often overly permissive and indulgent with their children during visits; but, after the first few months, their visits often decline in number, and many stop making child support payments (Hetherington, 1989).

4. Effects of Divorce on Children: Nearly one-third of American children live in single-parent households, and, of all single-parent families, the most common are those headed by divorced or separated mothers, although the number of father-headed households has increased.

The effects of divorce on children are usually most profound during the first year after the divorce. Common effects include increased misbehavior, aggression, and delinquency; lower academic achievement; problems related to psychological and emotional functioning; lowered self-esteem; and disruptions in interpersonal relationships (e.g., Amato, 2001). The consequences of divorce are affected by several factors, however, including those discussed below:

> *Child's age:* Children who are preschoolers at the time of the divorce initially exhibit more problems than older children, probably because they are less able to understand the reasons for divorce and are more likely to blame themselves and fear they will be abandoned by both parents. In contrast, the long-term consequences may be worse for

older children. Wallerstein (1987) found that children who were six to eight years old at the time of the divorce exhibited painful memories ten years later and feared they would have unsuccessful marriages themselves.

Child's gender: Research examining the relationship between gender and the effects of divorce has produced somewhat inconsistent results. Some studies show that boys are more adversely affected than girls and recover more slowly (Hetherington, 1989). Other research suggests that boys may show greater distress initially, but that the long-term consequences are similar for boys and girls so that, by adolescence, they are more similar in terms of severity of outcomes (Amato & Keith, 1991). The similarity of adolescent boys and girls may be due to a "sleeper effect" in which girls who do not initially show negative effects of the divorce develop a number of problems in adolescence including increased noncompliance and conflict with their mothers, antisocial behaviors, decreased self-esteem, and difficulties related to sexual behavior (e.g., Chase-Lansdale & Hetherington, 1990). As young adults, these girls are at high risk for becoming pregnant prior to marriage, choosing a husband who is psychologically unstable and economically insecure, and getting divorced themselves (Hetherington, 1988).

Custody arrangements: Several investigators report that children who live with the same-sex parent do better than those living with the opposite-sex parent – e.g., they have higher levels of self-esteem, lower anxiety and depression, and lower levels of antisocial behavior (e.g., Stevenson & Black, 1995). In contrast, Buchanan, Maccoby, and Dornbusch (1996) found that adolescent boys and girls living with their fathers had poorer adjustment and school grades than those living with their mothers, apparently due, in part, to the residential father's lack of monitoring of the teen's activities. Regardless of custody arrangements (whether the child is living with the same- or opposite-sex parent), adjustment outcomes are better when children have frequent, reliable contacts with the noncustodial parent. However, there is evidence that shared custody does not improve outcomes for children when the divorce is amicable and may actually worsen outcomes when the divorce is highly conflictual (Downey & Powell, 1993).

Conflict between the parents: There is evidence that boys with serious problems exhibited similar difficulties prior to their parents' divorce, apparently because the parents' marriage was a troubled one (Cherlin et al., 1991). This finding is consistent with studies showing that (a) there is not much difference between children of divorced parents and children of unhappily married parents (Wallerstein & Kelly, 1980); (b) conflictual intact families are more detrimental to a child's well-being than a stable single-parent or stepparent family (Demo & Acock, 1988); and (c) a lack of conflict is more important for a child's adjustment than the frequency of contact with the noncustodial parent (Amato & Rezac, 1994). These findings have led some experts to conclude that it is **parental conflict**, rather than divorce, that creates risk for children (Amato & Keith, 1991).

F. Remarriage, Stepparenting, and Blended Families

1. Children's Adjustment: The consequences of remarriage for children are similar to those following divorce, but the recovery period is often longer, particularly for older children and adolescents (Hetherington & Clingempeel, 1988). In general, following remarriage of their parents, children may develop behavioral or emotional problems as they adjust to new family roles (Heatherington & Stanley-Hagan, 2000). Behavioral problems are more common in boys, while girls often experience an increase in emotional problems. In addition, children's adjustment to their parents' remarriage is affected by the following factors:

Child's age: Younger children tend to be more accepting of a new adult in their lives (stepmother or stepfather), particularly if the new parent is a positive influence on the newly formed family. Adolescents, by contrast, tend to have more difficulties adjusting because they are moving toward independence: Younger adolescents (age 10 to 14) have the most difficult time adjusting because they are struggling with identity formation issues and tend to be oppositional; older adolescents (age 15 and up), on the other hand, need less parenting and are less invested in family life.

Child's gender: Girls, especially those in the middle-school years, appear to have more trouble than boys in accepting a stepfather, while the addition of a stepfather may have benefits for preadolescent boys. Over time, these boys often develop close relationships with their stepfathers and become fairly indistinguishable from boys in nondivorced families in terms of behavioral problems and academic achievement (Hetherington et al., 1985; Amato & Keith, 1991).

2. Stepparents' Adjustment: Stepparents frequently express concerns about their ability to discipline and provide affection to their stepchildren, and children confirm that stepparents (especially stepfathers) are less involved with them than their biological parents are. In fact, with regard to parenting, the best general conclusion that can be drawn about stepfathers is that they are more distant and disengaged than their biological counterparts (Hetherington, Bridges, & Insabella, 1998). There is also evidence that the parenting style adopted by a stepparent is an important determinant of the stepparent-stepchild relationship and the stepchild's adjustment: An authoritative parenting style has a positive effect, especially on the stepfather-stepson relationship; and, in general, the best outcomes occur when the stepparent is warm, involved, and supportive of the biological parent's authority (e.g., Hetherington, 1989).

3. The Blended Family: A blended family (also called a stepfamily or reconstituted family) is a family in which one or both members of the couple have children from a previous relationship. Wald (1989) encourages therapists to understand that the characteristics found in a typical stepfamily are not usually signs of pathological dynamics; rather, they reflect normal and transitional adjustments to a new situation. Even under the best conditions, it can take two to four years for the new family members to adjust to one another (Ganong & Coleman, 2003).

The parents in a newly blended family need to adapt to their marital relationship and help the children adjust to the family transition; some also need to continue relationships with ex-spouses. All members of a blended family need to accept losses and changes, adjust to role changes for all family members, and establish a lifestyle that successfully incorporates two households. Some members also need to readjust their expectations about what a family is.

G. Adoption

Adoption is a legal process that permanently gives parental rights to adoptive parents. Once an adoption is final, the adoptive parents have all the legal rights and responsibilities of a parent-child relationship. An adoptive parent can be a stepparent or domestic partner of one of the birth parents, a relative of the child who has been caring for the child, or someone not related to the child by blood.

Although some states have special requirements for adoptive parents (e.g., residency requirements), as a general rule, any adult who is determined to be a "fit parent" may adopt a child, even an adult who is unmarried. Unmarried couples are also permitted to adopt (this is sometimes called a "two-parent adoption"). Almost all states in the U.S. allow lesbians and gay men to adopt children, and an increasing number of states are allowing gay and lesbian couples to adopt jointly.

1. Arranging an Adoption: Adoptions can be arranged through an agency within a state's welfare department or Department of Children's Services, a private agency regulated by the state, or, in some states, a lawyer or physician. The latter are private adoptions in which the adoptive parents may receive less background information on the birth parents, and the birth mother usually receives less counseling. Private adoptions may also involve more legal problems than agency adoptions. Some adoption agencies will not arrange an adoption unless the birth mother identifies the baby's father so that his release can be obtained; some birth mothers, however, don't want to name the father either because they are afraid or because they don't want him to be involved.

2. Open Adoption: In open adoption, the birth mother (and, sometimes, the birth father) participates in selecting a family for the baby, the adoptive parent(s) may choose to be present at the baby's birth, and the birth mother may stay in contact with the family as the child grows up. Visits may be arranged between the birth mother and the child, sometimes through the adoption agency. Visitation may be limited to once or twice a year or the birth mother may see the child much more often, even serving sometimes as his babysitter. The research indicates that openly adopted children who maintain contact with their birth mothers usually view their adoptive mother as their mother, and their birth mother as an aunt or friend; very few experience confusion about who their "mother" is.

Open adoptions can lead to problems in some cases, however. For example, the birth mother may change her mind about the adoption after she gives birth, may unexpectedly cease contact with the child, or may place conditions on the adoption that affect the adoptive parents' parenting abilities and choices.

3. Adopting Children From Different Racial or Ethnic Backgrounds: Adoptive parents are not required to be of the same race or ethnic background as the child they want to adopt, but some agencies may give preference to prospective adoptive parents who are of the same racial or ethnic background as the child.

- The Multiethnic Placement Act of 1994 prohibits adoption decisions based solely on race, color, or national origin.

- The NASW's position is that efforts should be made to place a child in the home of parents who are of a similar racial and ethnic background; and the National Association of Black Social Workers (NABSW) is opposed to transracial adoptions and recommends that they be considered only as a last resort.

- The **Indian Child Welfare Act** (1978) gives tribes in the U.S. control over the adoption of Native American children. Adoptions involving Native American children require a release from both the birth parents and the tribe. The tribe may prohibit a non-Native

American family from adopting a Native American baby (even if the birth family has agreed to the adoption) and place the child with a Native American family. A tribe's rationale for this is usually that, to preserve their heritage, Native American children need to be raised by Native American families.

4. Adoption of Children With Special Needs: In the context of adoption, children with special needs are usually considered to be older children (commonly those over the age of 2 years but the age varies from state to state); children from racial or ethnic minorities; children who are members of a sibling group of two or more children; children with a physical or mental disability; children with an emotional disturbance; and children known to be at high risk for a physical or mental disease. Parents who adopt a child with special needs may receive a subsidy from their state to help cover certain expenses such as the cost of medical care.

Children who are being adopted from foster care are usually considered to be "special needs" children, as well. Children placed in foster care because of abuse or neglect may wait for years for their biological parents' parental rights to be terminated so that they can be put up for adoption. Although some people believe that abused children should be permanently removed from their parents' care and placed for adoption immediately, others support family-preservation efforts in which the ultimate goal is reuniting children with their biological families.

5. Home-Studies and Pre-Adoption Classes: In all states, individuals who apply to adopt a child are required by law to undergo a home-study. The home-study results in a written report prepared by a social worker who has met with the applicant(s). At least one meeting occurs in the applicants' home, and, if other people live in the home, they are also interviewed by the social worker. The home-study process and the contents of the written home-study report vary from state to state and agency to agency. In general, however, the following information is included in the home-study: personal and family background; significant people in the applicants' lives; marriage and family relationships; motivation to adopt; expectations for the child; feelings about infertility (if this is relevant); parenting and integration of the child into the family; family environment; physical and health history of the applicants; education; employment and finances (including insurance coverage and child-care plans, if needed); references and criminal background clearances; and the social worker's recommendations.

Each state also requires individuals who apply to adopt a child to attend pre-adoption classes. PACE (Partners in Alternative Care Education), for example, is a training program provided by a social worker and a foster parent. Other programs available in some states include Parents as Tender Healers (PATH) and Model Approach to Partnerships in Parenting (MAPP).

6. Adjustment of Adopted Children: The majority of adopted children do not develop notable, long-lasting psychological problems. Research on the adjustment of adopted children has shown the following:

- Adopted children who are separated from their initial caregivers before 3 months of age show little or no negative effects, but children separated at age 9 months or older often show moderate to severe reactions initially including social withdrawal, increased stranger anxiety, sleeping and feeding problems, and excessive clinging to the new mother or physical rejection of her (Yarrow & Goodwin, 1973).

- Longitudinal research (e.g., Hodges & Tizard, 1989) shows that "late adoptees" (those adopted after early infancy) have higher rates of emotional and behavioral problems, but that children initially raised in institutions are eventually able to develop a close bond with their adoptive parents if they are adopted by 6 years of age.

- At around age 5 to 7, some children adopted at a young age begin to display behavioral problems (acting out, aggression) as they start to understand that they are not living with their birth family.

7. Telling the Child He Was Adopted: Unless the adoption was open, adoptive parents face a decision as to whether and when to tell their child that he was adopted. The current recommendation is that adoptive parents be honest with the child from the beginning. In addition, laws are in place that permit adults who were adopted during childhood to obtain information about their birth parents if the birth parents did not request anonymity.

H. Foster Care

Foster care is full-time substitute care of a minor outside his own home by people other than his biological or adoptive parents or legal guardian. In all cases of foster care, the minor's biological or adoptive parents or other legal guardian temporarily give up legal custody of the minor, and the minor becomes a dependent of the court (or "ward of the court" in some states). When his or her child is placed in foster care, a legal guardian temporarily gives up legal custody but not necessarily legal guardianship.

1. Reasons Why Minors Are Placed in Foster Care: A minor may be placed in foster care with his parents' or legal guardian's consent. When a minor has been abused or neglected, however, a court can order the minor into foster care without his parents' or guardian's consent.

- Most minors are in foster care because they have experienced physical abuse, sexual abuse, or neglect at home.

- Other children enter foster care because of the absence of their parents or legal guardians due to illness, disability, or death.

- Other children enter foster care because of delinquent behavior or because they have committed a juvenile status offense, such as running away or truancy. In some cases, the parents feel unable to control their child and request that he be placed in foster care.

- Some minors are placed because their parents or legal guardians are unable to provide care as a result of substance abuse, mental health problems, or incarceration. These children may be placed into foster care while their parents or guardians receive treatment or counseling or complete their prison sentences.

2. Foster Care Settings: A child in foster care may be placed with relatives (kin placement); with non-relatives (e.g., family friends); in a group home where several foster children live together with a staff of caregivers; or in a foster home with other foster children, the family's biological or adoptive children, or alone. Group home foster care is more frequently used for older children. Children who have emotional, behavioral, physical, or medical needs and require a higher level of supervision and treatment may be placed in therapeutic foster care, residential child care, or residential psychiatric care. Therapeutic foster care may be provided in a group home or foster home.

A caseworker from a state or county child welfare agency oversees a child's placement and makes regular reports to the court. Other providers and resources that may be involved in the child's case include private service providers (including the foster home or group home), mental health counselors, substance abuse treatment centers (for the child or the parent), and Medicaid.

3. Foster Parents: Foster parents must be licensed by the agency that handles their region's foster care, and, in most states, foster parents are required to attend training sessions. When a minor is placed with them, the foster parents assume responsibility for feeding and clothing the minor, getting him to school and appointments, and doing other usual things that a minor's parents or legal guardians might be expected to do. The foster parents meet regularly with the minor's caseworker and may also meet with the minor's therapist. Foster parents do not become the legal guardians of foster children; instead, a child in foster care is in the custody of a child welfare agency (i.e., state custody) and is a dependent (or ward) of the court.

The specific areas explored when evaluating prospective foster parents include the following: (a) their health and mobility, (b) their views about child rearing, (c) their ability to accept responsibility, (d) their attitude toward the foster child's biological parents, (e) their motivation to foster a child who is not their own despite the temporary nature of the placement, (f) family composition and income, (g) suitability of accommodations, and (h) the general home environment. The foster home must pass an inspection for health and safety.

In terms of family medical issues, having a biological child with HIV disease cannot disqualify parents from being foster parents. In 2001, the U.S. Court of Appeals for the Third Circuit (Doe v. County of Centre, PA, et al.) ruled that a Pennsylvania county children's agency could not disqualify prospective foster parents just because one of their children had HIV disease or force them to disclose their children's health status.

4. Protections for Children in Foster Care: To receive Title IV-B funding for foster care (i.e., funding for child welfare services), states are required to provide certain protections to all children in foster care:

- Foster care placement must be consistent with the best interests and special needs of the child.

- Placements must be in the least restrictive environment, in the most family-like setting available, and in close proximity to the child's biological parents or legal guardians.

- There must be a detailed written case plan that describes the placement, the services provided to the child, and a plan for attaining permanence for the child, as well as a case review at least every six months. The review is used to determine whether the placement is still necessary and appropriate, whether the case plan is being properly and adequately followed, and whether progress has been made toward reunifying the family. The case review must also set a target date for the child's return home, adoption, or other permanent placement.

- The biological parents or legal guardians and the child must be allowed to participate in the development and approval of the case plan.
- A permanency planning hearing must be held for the child within 12 months of his initial placement or after a determination that reasonable efforts to reunite the family are not required or have been unsuccessful.

Other guidelines for children in foster care include the following (Fahlberg, 1991):

- Every effort should be made to stabilize placement for the child. Multiple placements place children at higher risk for adverse effects.
- Unless the biological parents or legal guardians are dangerous or there is no possibility of reuniting the family, the biological parents or legal guardians should visit the child in foster care so that the attachment is allowed to continue and the parents or guardians have the chance to practice positive interactions with the child.
- Whenever possible, siblings should be placed in the same foster home.
- Foster families should be made aware of a child's history so that they can be optimally responsive to the child's needs.

5. Permanency Planning and the Adoption Assistance and Child Welfare Act:
Permanency planning began as a movement in the 1970s that advocated either returning foster children to their biological homes or terminating parental rights and placing children for adoption. The movement led to the Adoption Assistance and Child Welfare Act of 1980, which mandated permanency planning for all states. **Permanency planning** seeks to provide alternatives to temporary foster care placement through organized efforts to provide long-term continuity in the care of dependent children. In theory, child welfare workers have always emphasized in-home supportive and supplementary services for children in foster care and their families (i.e., services that attempted to keep the child in his home and offer a permanent, nurturing relationship). The permanency planning movement helped change this theoretical emphasis into policy. Strategies used in permanency planning include helping a child's biological parents become able to care for the child, clarifying foster care guidelines, and assisting with adoptions.

The Adoption Assistance and Child Welfare Act emphasizes two goals for foster care. The first goal is to preserve the child's family, if at all possible. Ideally minors are placed in foster care only after other options have failed, and social service agencies work with the family to resolve its problems so that children can return to their homes. The second goal is to support permanency planning. For example, when a child must be removed from his home, the child welfare agency handling his case can determine quickly whether or not the child will ever be returned to his family. When it is very likely that his biological parents will not be able to care for him again, the agency can petition a court to terminate their parental rights so that the child can be free to be adopted.

6. Adjustment of Children in Foster Care: The majority of children in foster care enter care because of family dysfunction (e.g., abuse, neglect). Although removal from a dysfunctional family can have beneficial effects for a child, foster care placement is associated with an increased risk for certain medical, psychosocial, behavioral, and school problems. Many children remain in foster care for a long time waiting to return home to their biological parents or be placed for adoption. Some of these children are moved from one foster home to another. A lack of permanence and continuity of care can have adverse effects on a child.

- Children who experience multiple placements (are moved from one foster home to another) during the first several years of life are at higher-than-average risk for failure to thrive and attachment problems.

- The multiple losses experienced by foster children (e.g., family, peer relationships) can influence the way they view themselves, and, consequently, foster children are at risk for low self-esteem. This is particularly true for those who experience multiple placements or spend an extended period of time in foster care. Adolescents, for example, may have a difficult time forming a coherent identity if they are moved often from one foster home to another. On the other hand, removal of a child from a dysfunctional or violent family situation and placement in foster care, particularly stable placement in one home, can provide him with opportunities to develop supportive relationships that help him acquire a more positive image.

- Children who have been removed from their parents' home have suffered separation and loss and are likely to be feeling insecure and uncertain. They may blame themselves for the problems that led to their placement and feel as though they are being punished, and they often worry about the well-being of their parents. It is very common for children in foster care to have questions about their past, current situation, and future. Social workers should make it easy for foster children to ask these questions and, when responding, should be as factual and honest as possible.

IV. School and Worklife

A. School

1. Compensatory Preschool Programs: In general, children who attend preschool do not differ intellectually from those who stay at home during the preschool years. Exceptions to this general rule are children who attend **Head Start** and other compensatory preschool programs for economically disadvantaged children. While initial IQ test score gains produced by these programs are often not maintained and participants do not "catch up" to more advantaged children, there are other important benefits. For example, children who attend compensatory programs obtain higher scores on achievement tests, have better attitudes toward school, and are less likely to be retained in a grade, to be placed in special education classes, and to drop out of high school than their peers who do not attend such programs (Lazar et al., 1982). In addition, Barnett (1993) found that, 25 years after participation in a compensatory preschool program, participants exhibited benefits on a variety of life success measures including reduced rates of teen pregnancy, delinquency, unemployment, and reliance on welfare.

The positive effects of early compensatory education are enhanced when the programs are high in intensity in terms of amount of time that children spend in them; are coordinated with health, housing, and other social services; are followed by educational support once children have entered elementary school; and make use of carefully developed materials and procedures (Ramey & Ramey, 1990). In programs using the Montessori method, for example, the materials and environment are designed to fit the child's abilities, and learning is experiential with children receiving support and guidance from teachers that helps them advance at their own pace. Additionally, the Montessori method attempts to maximize learning by using instructional methods that are designed to enhance sense discrimination (i.e., that not only involve listening but also touching, seeing, smelling, and tasting).

2. Characteristics of Effective Schools: "Effective" schools have been defined as those that have higher standardized test scores, attendance rates, and student self-esteem and lower rates of delinquency. Key characteristics of effective schools include the following: (a) high standards and high expectations of academic achievement on the part of faculty; (b) classmates have a mixture of abilities and backgrounds (e.g., the academic performance of at-risk children may be adversely affected when they are separated from other children at school); (c) use of varied instructional techniques and methods, clear instructional objectives, activities tied to these objectives, and frequent monitoring and evaluation of student progress toward these objectives; (d) relatively little class time spent on discipline (teachers intervene early in potentially problematic situations); (e) safe and orderly (but nonrigid) school atmosphere; (f) strong leadership behavior by administrators, including the principal; and (g) involved parents.

3. School Phobia/School Refusal: School phobia (or school refusal) involves intense anxiety about going to school or being in school, usually accompanied by a stomachache, headache, nausea, and other physical symptoms. In many cases, either separation anxiety or a traumatic school experience underlies school phobia. When it leads to chronic absences from school, school phobia places children at risk for psychological problems later in life, such as alcohol abuse, criminal behavior, underemployment, and marital difficulties (Kearney, 2001).

School phobia/refusal often occurs at three different ages: at 5 to 7 years when the child first begins school; at 11 or 12 years when the child moves from elementary to middle school and when children tend to tease one another most viciously; and at 14 years or older. School refusal manifested between the ages of 5 and 7 is most likely due to separation anxiety; when it occurs during adolescence, it may be a sign of depression or another more serious disorder (Rosenhan & Seligman, 1984). In terms of intervention, many authorities agree that any intervention for school refusal should include an immediate return to school.

In terms of specific fears that children may have about school, some children experience generalized anxiety about their abilities, others fear specific school-related activities such as walking down the hallway, and others worry about their interactions with peers or fear speaking in public (the latter fears are associated with social anxiety disorder). Children most at risk for developing peer-related phobias are those who are harassed for physical traits (such as being overweight) or physical disabilities.

4. Elementary to Middle School Transition: For most youngsters, the transition from elementary school to middle school is stressful. It requires them to adapt to a larger, more impersonal school environment; to having multiple teachers and classrooms; and to no longer being the "top dog" (oldest, biggest, most powerful) at school. Some teens also lose supportive peer groups and teachers when they make this move. This transition can also be difficult because it coincides with the onset of puberty, which is associated with many additional changes (e.g., emerging body image concerns, reduced dependency on parents, changes in social cognition).

5. School Leavers (Dropouts): For most students, dropping out of school is not due to a lack of ability (i.e., school leavers generally have average intelligence scores). Instead, school leavers tend to be students who are disengaged from school. Studies have identified a number of factors that predict dropout, including poor attendance, disinterest in school, living in poverty, single-parent families, parents who do not participate in decision-making concerning the student, conduct problems in school, grade retention, poor grades, pregnancy, more than 15 hours of work per week, and an urban lifestyle (living in a city) (National Research Council, 1993a). Additionally, students of color are more likely than white students to drop out of high school; this has been attributed by some to poor academic preparation and disadvantaged economic backgrounds. Current dropout prevention efforts focus on schoolwide practices that reduce students' alienation from school and academics and increase their motivation and interest in learning.

6. Bilingual Education: Research on the effects of bilingual education has produced inconsistent results, partly because existing programs vary considerably in approach and quality. Probably the best overall conclusion that can be drawn is that, when language-minority children participate in high-quality bilingual programs, they acquire academic English and knowledge of subject matter as well as or better than those who participate in immersion (English-only) programs (Alkin, 1992; Rolstad, Mahoney, & Glass, 2005).

B. Worklife

"Jobs" and "careers" differ. Often a job is simply a way of earning a living, and it may not have much meaning to a person from a psychological perspective. A career, by contrast, is more likely to be a central part of a person's identity. People often pursue careers as a way of life rather than just as a means of earning an income. Not everyone has an opportunity to pursue a career.

1. Working Women: Employed women are generally more satisfied with their lives than nonemployed women, although this may be true only for employed women who want to work outside the home (Grove & Zeiss, 1987). It has been suggested that women may be less happy when they occupy the "homemaker" role because this role continues to carry a negative connotation in our society, so that the status of the homemaker is low. In addition, women who don't work outside the home may be socially isolated.

a. Effects of Maternal Employment on Husbands/Fathers and Marriages: There is some evidence that personal and marital satisfaction are lower among men holding traditional sex-role stereotypes, but, overall, there seems to be no consistent relationship between maternal employment and the father's sense of well-being or the marital satisfaction of either partner (Warr & Perry, 1982). With regard to the division of labor, working mothers continue to be responsible for the majority of childcare and other household tasks, but several recent studies indicate that men in dual-earner couples are assuming more responsibility for household chores than they did in the past.

b. Effects of Maternal Employment on Children: The results of the research on this topic have been mixed, but the best conclusion is probably that the benefits outweigh the costs: Children of working women have more egalitarian gender-role concepts and more positive views of femininity, and daughters have higher levels of self-esteem, independence, and achievement motivation, and higher career goals (Hoffman, 1989). Some studies suggest that, in lower-SES (socioeconomic status) families, sons of working mothers obtain higher scores on measures of cognitive development, but, in higher-SES families, they may obtain lower scores on achievement and IQ tests (Hoffman, 1989; Greenstein, 1993). There is also evidence that maternal employment is most likely to have negative outcomes for boys (e.g., lower school achievement, more behavioral problems, and increased mother-child conflict) when it is combined with low levels of parental supervision and monitoring (Crouter et al., 1990). Finally, maternal employment is less likely to have a negative impact on children if both parents have a positive attitude toward it (Belsky & Rovine, 1988; Spitze, 1988).

2. Young Adulthood – Entering the Workforce: Beginning in young adulthood, a person's work can become a significant aspect of his identity. To adjust successfully to the workplace, young people need to adapt to various components that are specific to their particular job or career – these may include the use of certain technical skills, relationships with those in authority, and interpersonal relationships with coworkers (Newman & Newman, 2002). Additionally, a young adult who is starting a family must learn how to achieve a suitable balance among his work, family life, and leisure activities.

3. Middle Adulthood – Career Satisfaction and Change: By midlife, work may be even more personally meaningful and provide an even greater level of personal satisfaction than before (Lemme, 2001).

a. Midlife Career Change: About 10 percent of men and women make a career change at midlife. Newman and Newman (2002) have identified reasons why a person's work-related goals may change: (a) Some careers end in middle adulthood because the person can no longer perform the requisite duties (e.g., professional athlete). (b) Some people decide at midlife that their work is no longer meaningful to them and seek a more meaningful career. (c) Some people believe they have succeeded as much as they can in their current job (e.g., they would need specialized training to keep up with the job). (d) Women may change careers after their children are "launched" because they have more time to devote to work. (e) Some people change careers because of economic pressures that require a restructuring of the workforce and the layoff of some workers. Additionally, some midlife women (as well as some older or younger women) become **displaced homemakers** – they are forced into the job market by circumstances of divorce or widowhood.

b. Women and Interrupted Careers: Many middle-aged women have careers that began before motherhood, got interrupted by childrearing, and were then reestablished when they resumed full-time work after their children left home. This work pattern affects a woman's career progress and financial security later in life (i.e., retirement income is directly related to work history). Additionally, a midlife woman's renewed focus on career may lead to conflict in her marriage or family (i.e., she may place less emphasis than before on her roles at home). A couple's ability to adapt to this situation depends on how the husband views women's participation in the workforce (e.g., does he consider his career more important than his wife's?), on how the partners go about resolving changes in their roles, and on the flexibility with which they approach change.

c. Men and the Career/Family Balance: In middle adulthood, spouses may be in conflict over the amount of time the husband spends working. Even men who believe that their contribution to the family should involve more than financial support may have difficultly working less while still retaining their sense of being "manly." This is because men tend to gain a significant part of their personal identity from what they do (e.g., they may express their manhood through work). On the other hand, some midlife men do begin questioning not only their status at work (e.g., is my work meaningful?) but also their contribution to the family (e.g., a midlife man may regret not having spent more time with his children). These competing issues can make it difficult for a midlife man to find a comfortable balance between work and family life.

4. Late Adulthood – Work and Retirement: Because the U.S. no longer has mandatory retirement laws (Age Discrimination in Employment Amendments of 1986), older adults can work for as long as they want to, and some work well into their 70s or 80s. People over age 65 who continue to work tend to be well educated and to hold relatively flexible jobs with moderate levels of stress and high satisfaction (Meadows, 2003). This includes many older people who are self-employed.

a. Phases of Retirement: Retirement involves a significant shift in a person's family roles, daily activity, social interactions, and financial resources. How a person anticipates these changes can affect how successfully he retires. Atchley (1976) has characterized retirement as a process with several phases:

Preretirement – people imagine their retirement and make plans for it.

Honeymoon – the time just after retirement; most people savor their newfound freedom and experience a sense of greater well-being.

Disenchantment – satisfaction with retirement begins to level off and retirement eventually seems less pleasant than before.

Reorientation – the person becomes more realistic about retirement and learns to make the necessary adaptations (e.g., he finds new part-time or full-time work, starts volunteering, takes up a new hobby). Eventually, the person establishes a routine in which retirement becomes the normal way of life.

Research by Kim and Moen (2002) found that Atchley's stages appear to apply well to men, but that for women there is no consistent difference in their well-being from early to later retirement.

b. Retirement Satisfaction (Well-Being After Retirement): Male and female retirees who participate in productive or fulfilling activities (e.g., paid work, volunteering, caregiving) are more likely to be satisfied during retirement than those who are inactive. The likelihood of **retirement satisfaction** is highest for people who participate in two or more activities. Studies also show that retired older people who are active have better physical and mental health, better cognitive and social functioning, and lower mortality rates (Fried et al., 2004). Volunteering, for example, provides an older adult with a meaningful social role, which can enhance his life satisfaction. For men and women, other factors predictive of retirement satisfaction include health status, perceived income adequacy, and the ability to formulate an adequate new identity (Kim & Moen, 2002; Barnes & Parry, 2004).

c. Living on a Fixed Income: Many older retired people live on fixed incomes (their income doesn't increase each year), which usually means that they must change their lifestyles every year or so to cope with fewer financial resources. For some, these adjustments have few adverse effects on their lives. For others, these adjustments require such changes as eating less food or doing without heat or air-conditioning. Even people who saved money for retirement may find their finances depleted if they or a family member experiences serious illness. Older people who fall into poverty often stay in poverty because they have low or no potential for future earning. Older women are more likely than older men to live in poverty (AARP, 2003), particularly women of color and women who worked at low-paying jobs or jobs that did not provide Social Security benefits. Even if these women are eligible to receive other public benefits, the amount they receive is usually very low (Ashford et al., 2006).

V. Group Theory and Dynamics

A group is a social system with regular interaction among the members and a common group identity. People generally join groups voluntarily to achieve one or more of the following goals: to meet their need for affiliation, to increase their sense of identity and self-esteem, to obtain a source for social comparison between themselves and others, to gain a greater sense of security and power, or to accomplish a specific task or tasks (Schein, 1980).

Participation in a group can affect individuals in a number of different ways, including the following: Through direct instruction, feedback, and modeling, groups can provide members with task-related or interpersonal skills. Groups can also satisfy members' affiliative needs, especially when members share interests and values. Finally, groups can also reduce a member's anxiety.

1. Stages of Group Development: Regardless of their purpose, groups typically go through several predictable stages of development. One model, developed by Tuckman and Jensen (1977), describes the stages of group development in the following way:

Stage 1 – Forming: Members become acquainted with one another and attempt to establish ground rules with respect to both the task and interpersonal relationships. In groups with a designated leader, the members may communicate primarily through the leader, rather than directly with each other, during this stage.

Stage 2 – Storming: This stage is marked by a high degree of conflict as members resist the control of the group leader and act hostilely toward one another. This stage must be successfully resolved in order for the group to move on to the next stage of its development.

Stage 3 – Norming: The group becomes more cohesive and individuals identify themselves as members of the group. Feelings of camaraderie, friendship, and shared responsibility develop.

Stage 4 – Performing: This stage is devoted to achieving the group's tasks and goals.

Stage 5 – Adjourning: The group disbands when the group's goals have been met or when many of the group's members have left.

2. Group Norms: Norms are the standard rules of conduct that are used by groups to maintain uniformity of behavior among group members. Norms may be formal (codified or written) or informal (unwritten, but "understood" by group members). Norms do not govern all aspects of behavior; they govern only those behaviors considered by the group's members to be important for effective group functioning. In addition, norms usually apply to behavior only, not to personal feelings and thoughts. Several conditions contribute to a group member's conformity to group norms:

Task demands: Conformity to group norms tends to be greater in ambiguous situations, highly complex situations, and situations involving a problem that has no solution. Conformity is also high when group members must work together in order to achieve a common goal.

Group characteristics: Conformity increases as the unanimity (consensus) of group members increases. The presence of even a single dissenter can significantly lower conformity. A high degree of conformity is also likely when the group uses surveillance or close supervision to enforce its norms and when group members are perceived as being highly credible and trustworthy.

Individual characteristics: High levels of conformity are associated with authoritarianism, rigidity, and low self-esteem, while low levels of conformity are associated with high intelligence, tolerance, and ego strength. Members also conform more to a group's norms when they have helped to define those norms.

3. Group Cohesion: Cohesion refers to a group's solidarity. High cohesiveness has been linked to more frequent communication among group members, greater participation in group activities, reduced conflict, and higher levels of morale, interpersonal attraction, and conformity. Factors determining a group's level of cohesiveness include the following:

Group size: The optimal group size depends on the nature of the task, but, in general, groups are more effective when they include five to ten members. Smaller groups tend to be more cohesive than larger groups, and they ordinarily have fewer communication problems, less member dissatisfaction and alienation, less need for supervision and surveillance, and more per-capita communication and productivity. As groups get larger, subgroups (cliques) tend to form, communication becomes more formalized, and leadership becomes more autocratic.

Homogeneity: Groups whose members are similar in terms of socioeconomic status, interests, values, attitudes, abilities, and personality characteristics are more likely to be cohesive. Group homogeneity is also associated with greater member satisfaction in socially oriented groups and greater productivity in task-oriented groups when the task is simple. When the task requires originality and creativity, however, greater productivity is associated with heterogeneity.

Goals: Cohesiveness is maximized when members participate in goal- (and norm-) setting and when members must depend on one another to achieve their common goals. Cohesiveness is also increased when members believe that participation in the group will help them achieve their own personal goals and when the group has a previous history of successful goal achievement.

Difficult entry into the group: Difficult application procedures and severe initiations are associated with greater cohesiveness.

External threat: The presence of competition or other external threat tends to increase group interdependence and cohesiveness.

4. Potential Liabilities in Group Decision-Making: In many situations, group decisions are better than decisions made by individuals. In some situations, however, groups produce less than optimal decisions:

Groupthink: Janis (1982) described **groupthink** as a suspension of critical thinking that can occur in highly cohesive groups, especially when the leader is highly directive and the group is working under conditions of high stress. According to Janis, groups engaging in groupthink are characterized by an illusion of invulnerability and unanimity, collective rationalization, unquestioned morality, excessive negative stereotyping, strong pressure to conform, self-appointed "mindguards," and self-censorship of dissenting views. A group leader can reduce the likelihood of groupthink by encouraging skepticism and dissent among group members, appointing someone to play devil's advocate, bringing in outside opinions, reducing time pressures to reach a solution, and not stating his own opinion prior to a group discussion.

Group polarization: **Group polarization** refers to the tendency for groups to make decisions that are more extreme in the direction of the views initially held by group members than the decisions that would have been generated by individual members alone. Group polarization has been attributed to several factors including the effects of social comparison, mutual reinforcement, and diffusion of responsibility. A shift in the direction of riskiness is also known as the **risky shift phenomenon**.

VI. Community Functioning and Development

A. Community Characteristics and Functions

A community is a social system that has a consciously identified population organized in pursuit of common goals. It includes a combination of social units and systems that perform major social functions relevant to meeting people's needs on a local level.

1. Types of Communities (Fellin, 2001): Most traditional definitions of community emphasize the concept of space or place, but, as shown below, communities may also be "nonplace."

Geographical (spacial or territorial) community: This is a community bounded by a geographically defined perimeter (i.e., a "place" community). Examples include a neighborhood, town, or city. Geographical communities vary in how they meet their residents' needs and in how social interactions are patterned and collective identity is perceived.

Community of identification and interest: This is a nongeographical (nonplace) community in which people are united by common interests, values, and commitments or brought together based on their shared ethnicity, race, religion, sexual orientation, social class, ideology, lifestyle, profession, or workplace. Other names for this type of community include "**functional community**," "relational community," "associational community," and "community of affiliation." Social workers, for example, belong to the "welfare or human services functional community." The beliefs and values of one functional community may conflict with those of another (e.g., while the social work professional community believes in advocacy for the poor, a political community may want to reduce government spending and public assistance).

Collective relationships of an individual: This is the set of relationships of an individual that gives him a sense of meaning and identity (e.g., his friends, neighbors, and coworkers). In a complex society, people establish networks of informal and formal relationships based on both place and nonplace considerations. Some people find their sense of community through dispersed relationships in which members rarely meet. When this is the case, social workers may have difficulty mobilizing people to address a local community problem.

2. Community Functions: Communities perform specific functions for their members. In "ideal" communities, these functions are carried out in a way that meets the needs of every member. Almost all communities are "dysfunctional" or "incompetent" to some degree, however, meaning that these functions are carried out in a way that doesn't meet the needs of at least some residents, usually the members of oppressed populations. Warren (1978) has identified five functions carried out by communities (these functions may also be performed by neighborhoods):

Production, distribution, and consumption of goods and services: These are activities designed to meet residents' material needs, including basic needs for food, clothing, and shelter, as well as medical care, sanitation, employment, transportation, recreation, etc.

Socialization: This refers to the transmission of values, culture, beliefs, and norms to new members. Socialization occurs through both formal (laws, rules, procedures) and informal (e.g., other community members' reactions) mechanisms and guides attitudinal development. These attitudes then influence how people view themselves, others, and their interpersonal rights and responsibilities.

Social control: Community members promote compliance with norms and values by establishing laws, rules, and regulations and systems for their enforcement. Social control maintains the reliability of a community, which gives residents a sense of security. Some forms of social control are overt (e.g., the enforcement of laws), while others are more subtle (e.g., patterns of service distribution and eligibility criteria that control access to resources).

Social participation: Communities provide opportunities (e.g., churches, civic organizations, informal neighborhood groups) for residents to express their social needs and interests and build natural helping and support networks. Understanding the opportunities and patterns of social participation is helpful in assessing the extent to which a community is meeting the needs of its members.

Mutual support: Within a community, family members, partners, friends, neighbors, volunteers, and professionals care for residents who are sick, unemployed, distressed, etc. As communities have become more complex, traditional institutions such as families and neighbors have had more difficulty fulfilling this function on their own.

Building on Warren's work, Pantoja and Perry (1992) identified two other functions carried out by communities – defense and communication. "Defense" refers to how a community takes care of and protects its members and is particularly important in communities that are unsafe. The defense function also applies to nonplace communities (e.g., the gay and lesbian community). "Communication" refers to the use of a common language and symbols to express ideas and connects people to each other. In modern communities, the important role of language is demonstrated by debates over political correctness and English-only initiatives. According to Pantoja and Perry, all other community functions (including those described by Warren) depend on production, distribution, and consumption – when a community lacks a stable economic base, its other functions, which are primarily supportive, are impaired and the community becomes dysfunctional.

B. Community Concepts and Theories

1. Simple Needs and Collective Needs: Within a community, *simple needs* are those experienced by a relatively small number of residents – when the needs of a few individuals are not met by available resources, there is a community problem that requires a social service response.

With *collective needs*, a community's basic service and support systems are failing to provide a minimally acceptable quality of life for all or most residents. For collective needs, a social service response (e.g., more resources) provides only a temporary solution because it doesn't address fundamental structural problems. Collective needs should be addressed through encouraging community members' participation in decisions that affect their lives, redesign of structures and systems, etc. For some collective needs, intervention has to occur at a level outside the immediate community, such as via the state legislature or federal government.

2. Horizontal and Vertical Community Linkages: The concepts of horizontal and vertical community linkages (Warren, 1978) highlight the complex interactions that can exist within a community and between a community and the larger society. The *horizontal community* consists of linkages between and among organizations and neighborhoods that are located within the same geographic region and usually serve the community. Elements of a horizontal community (schools, libraries, etc.) may collaborate to resolve a local problem.

Horizontal relationships are complemented by vertical relationships in which communities connect outside their geographical boundaries: Vertical, or external, linkages connect community units (people, groups, organizations) to units outside the community and provide a way for local communities to reach out to other systems, including groups, organizations, and other communities. The concept of *vertical community* highlights the fact that important decisions may be made by organizations outside the boundaries of a local community, and these decisions may not always be in the best interests of the community.

3. Tönnies's Concepts: Tönnies's work is the foundation from which community theory developed in the 1900s. His concepts of Gemeinschaft and Gesellschaft (1887) remain useful for understanding the concept of community and highlight the differences between informal and formal systems:

- **Gemeinschaft**, which means "community," focuses on intimacy and relationship. It emphasizes the mutual, common, and intimate bonds that bring people together in local units. These bonds are based on caring about one another and valuing the relationships in the group; the group is valued whether or not its members are creating a product or achieving a goal. Examples include the household unit, neighborhood, and groups of friends.
- **Gesellschaft** refers to society or association (e.g., the city or state). It represents the formalized, task-oriented relationships in which people organize to achieve a purpose, goal, or task. People may benefit from these relationships but their purpose is to create a product, achieve a goal, or complete a task.

4. Community as a Social System: Because a community is a social system, it has characteristics found in all systems, including the following:

Boundaries: Communities are separated from their environment by political, physical, or psychological boundaries.

Boundary maintenance: Boundary maintenance is necessary for system survival – if boundaries become blurred or indistinguishable, the community becomes less vital.

Homeostasis: Like other systems, communities tend to respond to change by seeking homeostasis and attempting to maintain the status quo when threatened by external stressors that disrupt equilibrium.

Task and maintenance functions: Communities seek to maintain a variety of services, meet the needs of multiple groups, and respond to special interest groups. Examples of task functions are police and fire protection. Maintenance functions are primarily social and serve to maintain the identity and well-being of communities (e.g., recreational facilities).

Subsystems: A community is a collection of subsystems that perform functions for its members (e.g., economic, political, health, education, and social welfare subsystems). A community's subsystems interact with and influence each other and other systems inside and outside the community.

5. Anomie: Anomie refers to a condition arising when the values, norms, and codes of behavior in a community, society, etc., have been either weakened or eradicated; when anomie is present, individuals are commonly alienated and apathetic and have lost sight of their goals. Anomie often is found in rapidly changing communities or ones that are experiencing extreme stress.

A related concept is **social capital**, which refers to the set of values, beliefs, and behaviors that are followed by the members of a society and that contribute to the well-being of all. Social capital tends to be higher when people's sense of community is strong.

6. Social Structural Theory: Social structural theory focuses on understanding how various subsystems in a community (or other system) affect the individual and the group. Emphasis is placed on how some social structures (systems) empower people and others oppress them.

7. Functionalism: "Functionalism" proposes that social structures (i.e., social entities that exist in relationship to other structures) and social function (i.e., the roles, purposes, and uses of the entities) in a social system are "inextricably intertwined" (Harrison, 1995, p. 556). In other words, structures (e.g., schools) are intermeshed with functions (teaching) and understanding community requires analysis of structures and functions together, not as separate entities.

8. Human or Population Ecology Theory: "Human ecology" examines the structural patterns and relationships within place-based communities. Contemporary ecological theorists focus on population demographics (e.g., age, gender, race), the use of physical space, and the structures and technology within communities. Recognizing how the use of physical space can either improve or diminish access to community resources is important, particularly in communities with diverse population groups.

a. View of Competent Communities: For human ecologists, communities are highly interdependent and filled with changing relationships among populations of people and organizations: "... [A] competent community enjoys a productive balance between its inhabitants and their environment, allowing for change in an orderly, nondestructive manner and providing essential daily sustenance requirements for its citizens" (Fellin, 1995, p. 11).

b. The Functioning of Place-Based Communities: Human ecologists focus on how place-based communities handle the processes of competition, centralization, concentration, integration, and succession (Fellin, 2001):

Competition vs. cooperation: In human ecology theory, degree of competition is primarily related to the acquisition or possession of land among competing groups; and competition changes from low to intense depending on power dynamics. There may also be competition among community groups all seeking to have their needs considered more important than others' needs (e.g., competition for resources and attention). This competition is largely a political activity in which many valid needs compete with other equally valid needs.

Centralization vs. decentralization: This describes the extent to which groups and organizations (e.g., business services) cluster in one location or disperse beyond the local area.

Concentration vs. dispersion: Concentration is a process in which people enter communities via migration or immigration. Communities vary from large to small depending on how many people or organizations remain within a particular locale.

Integration vs. segregation (of population groups): This continuum develops as diverse groups either maintain or reduce their separation by characteristics such as race, religion, age, etc.

Succession vs. status quo: This refers to the degree of community change (succession), or the speed at which one social group (e.g., residents) or set of organizations replaces another within the geographical area.

c. *Invasion and Gentrification:* Two other significant processes in place-based communities are invasion and gentrification. *Invasion* is the tendency of each new group of arrivals (primarily residents) to force out existing groups previously living in a neighborhood. Invasion also occurs when land-use patterns change (e.g., large single-family homes are converted into apartments). *Gentrification*, which is a corollary of invasion, occurs when upper middle-class families move back into downtown residential areas, converting upper floors of businesses into lofts or rehabilitating older homes.

9. Human Behavior Theories: The various human behavior theories focus on how people behave in communities (i.e., how they perceive and find meaning in relationships, what values guide their actions, and how their needs are determined).

a. *Collective Identity – The Sociopsychological Perspective:* This view contends that "community" is a sense of solidarity based on psychological identification with others – that is, community is more than social interaction; it is rooted in a sense of "we-ness" that can be place specific or transcend place (Clark, 1973).

b. *Diversity Functions:* MacNair, Fowler, and Harris (2000) identify six functions (approaches to change in communities) that demonstrate how different people may identify with nonplace communities for different purposes:

Assimilation: With assimilation, identity is connected to mainstream culture. Change is intended to allow the individual to become a part of existing, oppressive communities in which he has previously been denied access.

Normative nondiscrimination: This is a confrontational approach that stays within legal boundaries and is used to gain access to community institutions that are oppressive.

Militant direct action: This approach attempts to catch people off guard through activism. The goal of change is to gain a place within the community for people involved in the movement.

Separatism: In this approach, parallel communities are formed, identity becomes tied to the alternative community, interaction with the mainstream community is distressing, and norms develop among members of the oppressed community and may be hidden from the mainstream.

Introspective self-help: This approach is used when separatism is difficult to maintain and community members must focus on self-development and self-mastery.

Pluralistic integration: With pluralistic integration, groups confident in their own cultural identities retain their distinctiveness. They participate among and with persons from other cultures without losing their own identity.

c. *Values and the Relational Perspective:* According to Cohen (1985), community boundaries are not necessarily connected to place. Instead, "community" is filled with values, symbols, and ideologies that people have in common and that distinguish them from those who hold different beliefs; thus, boundaries may be racial, ethnic, linguistic, religious, or perceptual. The commonality in a relational community does not have to be uniformity, however; it can be a commonality of forms (ways of behaving) whose contents (meanings) may vary among its members. Cohen further maintains that the clarity of boundaries is not important because boundaries often change. Rather, he stresses the "symbolic aspect of community boundary" (p. 12); for example, even when people move out of a community, they retain the symbols, values, and ideologies they used with others in that community as symbols of their close relationship.

10. Empowerment, Resiliency, and Strengths Perspectives: Saleeby (1997) believes that the concepts of empowerment, resilience, and membership can inspire a community. *Empowerment* means helping communities recognize the resources they have; *resilience* refers to the potential emerging from the energy and skills needed to solve problems; and *membership* refers to the fact that being part of a community brings civic and moral strength.

- An **empowerment perspective** assumes that individuals, groups, and communities have the capacity to gain control over decisions that affect them if they recognize how social structures influence everything they do (i.e., when people are excluded from decisions and resources go only to those with power, leadership can emerge and promote an understanding of how decisions can be controlled locally). According to Gutierrez and Lewis (1999), empowerment practice should focus on three levels: personal, interpersonal, and political.

- The **resiliency perspective** assumes that communities have the potential to rebound and cope. Breton (2001) associates resilience with neighborhoods: "The stock of human and social capital characteristic of resilient neighborhoods consists of neighborhood networks and the trust they generate, active local voluntary associations through which residents mobilize for action, stable local organizational networks, and the services typical of an adequate social infrastructure" (p. 22).

- When applied to communities, the **strengths perspective** (Saleeby, 1997) focuses on a community's assets rather than its deficits or limitations and emphasizes the importance of recognizing, assessing, and using a community's strengths. **Asset mapping** (Kretzmann & McKnight, 1993) is a method that can be used to identify a community's strengths so that solutions then arise from the community itself rather than from "services."

11. Communitarianism: The communitarian movement has been influenced by postmodernism, feminist theory, and concerns about the weakening of communities in the

United States. Its advocates, such as Etzioni (1993), stress the influence of social policies on how people work together in a community and the importance of focusing on the collective rather than on the individual. In promoting the return to local control and responsibility, Etzioni writes, "The government should step in only to the extent that other social subsystems fail, rather than seek to replace them ... at the same time, vulnerable communities should be able to draw on the more endowed communities when they are truly unable to deal, on their own, with social duties thrust upon them" (p. 260).

C. Power, Conflict, and Politics in Communities

Barker (2003) defines power as, "the possession of resources that enables an individual to do something independently or to exercise influence and control over others" (p. 333). In a community, sources of power include financial assets, business ownership, community status, possession of information, or links to other individuals, groups, or organizations. One person may have multiple sources of power.

Community power may be viewed from three different perspectives (Meenaghan & Gibbons, 2000):

- An *elitist approach* assumes that a small number of people have disproportionate power in various community sectors.

- A *pluralist approach* implies that, as issues change, various interest groups and changing coalitions arise.

- An *amorphous structure* implies no persistent pattern of power relationships within the community.

1. Power Acquisition Theories:

a. Conflict Theory: **Conflict theory** suggests that human behavior in social contexts results from conflicts between competing groups, and that, while different social groups have unequal power, all groups struggle for the same limited resources.

The key assumptions of conflict theory include the following (Hardina, 2002):

- **Conflict** is the norm in social life (i.e., social life produces opposition, exclusion, and hostility; and social systems are neither united nor harmonious).

- Conflict is not necessarily a sign of instability, and, when harnessed properly, it can be used to bring about social change.

- A community is divided into "haves" and "have-nots" competing for scarce resources (i.e., "haves" and "have-nots" have conflicting interests).

- **Oppression** arises primarily from "isms" (racism, classism, etc.) (i.e., people are usually oppressed because of prejudice and discrimination).

- Conflict involves a struggle over values and competing claims to limited resources in which opponents seek to neutralize, harm, or eliminate their rivals. Thus, social life involves **competition** for resources. Competition unbalances society until a dominant group gains control and stability through power.

- **Power** is defined as the ability to control and influence collective decisions and actions.

- There are three kinds of power (Mills, 1967): *Authority* involves power that is justified by the beliefs of those who are voluntarily obedient; *manipulation* is power that is exercised without the knowledge of those who are oppressed; and *coercion* (the "final" form of power) occurs when the powerless are forced to obey the powerful. According to Collins (1974), coercion (the ability to force others to behave in a certain way) is the primary basis of conflict.

- "Haves" hold power over "have-nots."

- Government and other decision-making entities are controlled by "haves." The **power elite** enact policies that serve their own interests. Government planners, in turn, "rubber stamp" these policies in order to maintain the status quo.

According to the neo-Marxist view of conflict theory, social services perform a social control function in which just enough resources are provided to prevent people from protesting and to maintain the status quo. While that view seems to place social workers in the role of social control agents, Alinsky (1971) maintains that a key role of social workers is to organize to use power in ways that upset those in critical decision-making positions. In this context then, social workers applying conflict theory serve as advocates, agitators, negotiators, and partisans, and their goal is to shift the power of relationships and resources and, thereby, bring about institutional change. For example, community organizers work with oppressed groups to help them find sources of power and gain a voice in community decision-making.

b. Power Dependency Theory: This theory assumes that organizations and communities are dependent on donors and that external funders may make demands that limit a community's ability to initiate change, that consumers may limit change in order to avoid offending funders, and that community members may feel obligated to agree with donors.

c. Resource Mobilization Theory: Resource mobilization theory draws from the above two theories and focuses on social movements and why they happen. It assumes that social movements (mobilization) need a collective identity. Basic assumptions of **resource mobilization** as it applies to community practice include the following: (a) social movements emerge when groups are not represented in decision-making processes (these groups initiate social movements); (b) public protest brings public recognition to an issue; (c) movements need structure; (d) a movement's success depends on a collective identity for those involved in the protest; (e) the strength of a movement depends on the quality of the message; and (f) it can be difficult to acquire funding for a movement without compromising the group's (often radical) position.

2. Conflict and the Dual Perspective: According to the dual perspective (Norton, 1978), an individual exists in a nurturing system that functions within a larger sustaining system. The nurturing system immediately surrounds the individual and includes the traditions and informal relationships that are most familiar and comfortable to him (relationships within his family, support networks, and neighborhood). The sustaining system is composed of the beliefs, values, traditions, and practices of the dominant society (e.g., economic, political, legal, and educational systems). Conflict, tension, alienation, and deflated self-esteem can result if there is an incongruence between the values and beliefs represented by a person's nurturing system and those of the sustaining system (such an incongruence is most likely to occur among minority populations and recent immigrants). For people who experience *incongruence* between their nurturing and sustaining systems, issues such as community politics, power, and change are part of their day-to-day experience. People who experience *congruence*, on the other hand, may have a false sense that their community is supportive of all of its members.

3. Community Political Systems:

a. Levels of Government: Three levels of government affect decisions in a community:

- The federal government funds social programs, protects civil rights, and may act in partnership with state government (e.g., the Personal Responsibility and Work Opportunity Reconciliation Act established rules that govern whether states qualify for certain federal welfare funding, but, after these rules are met, states may develop their own policies for specific programs).

- The state government funds a significant portion of health and mental health services, provides financial support for local school districts, and enforces rules regarding how these monies are spent.

- The local (county or city) government may provide health and social services and offers fire and police services.

b. Governmental Functions in a Community: Governmental functions in a community include, among others, designing community programs; allocating funds (e.g., for homeless shelters, general assistance); providing services for citizens (e.g., fire, police); awarding and supervising contracts (e.g., a contract with a private social service agency to provide needed social services); determining and enforcing laws and regulations (housing, sanitation, health, etc.); mediating disputes (landlord and tenant, etc.); and planning for the community.

c. Formal/Official and Informal Political Systems: At the community level, the political system includes both formal organizations (e.g., city government where funding decisions are made) and informal political processes and activities. The political system may either encourage or discourage the participation of community residents (especially minorities) in decision-making.

Formal/official: Formal political systems include elected officials, the city bureaucracy, staff who carry out city functions, and appointed committees who advise elected officials. Formal citizen involvement may occur through organizations such as the Chamber of Commerce.

Informal citizen involvement: Community members (including those who are part of the power structure) may use their personal power and influence. A community's power structure is comprised of business leaders and others who have significant influence over what happens in the community including decisions made by government officials. A community's power structure usually exists outside the formal government structure (its members are not elected or accountable to community members).

d. Citizen Participation Roles in Communities: According to Burke (1968), citizen participation roles in communities include the following:

- *Review proposals for change.* This is the most limited role, and citizen comments may or may not be incorporated. Review processes may be carried out in committee meetings or public hearings.

- *Consultation.* This involves giving opinions on a proposed change when asked.

- *An advisory role.* This involves a formal mechanism such as a standing planning committee whose members advise decision-makers on factors affecting a target population. Although advisory committees don't have the power of policy boards, they can have a strong influence because they have access to decision-makers.

- *Shared decision-making.* This is a stronger role than advising and places citizens and consumers in roles where they can, in collaboration with professionals and community leaders, affect decisions.

- *Controlled decision-making.* This places citizens and consumers in positions of control over decisions such as policy statements through membership on review boards or boards of directors. These positions allow for the greatest amount of control by citizens and consumers.

VII. Understanding the Influence of Diversity

Culture is defined as, "... the customs, habits, skills, technology, arts, values, ideology, science, and religious or political behavior of a group of people in a specific time period" (Barker, 2003, p. 105). In the United States, the dominant, or mainstream, culture is characterized principally by the worldview (values, beliefs, attitudes) of middle-class white-Anglo men and women. This is true despite the significant presence of many other cultural, ethnic, racial, and class groups in our nation.

A. Prejudice, Discrimination, Oppression, and Racism

Prejudice is an *attitude* that has an affective component (the prejudice itself) and a cognitive component (stereotypes); it may also have a behavioral component (discrimination). **Discrimination** refers to *behaviors* such as unequal treatment (as noted above, prejudice is an *attitude* that may or may not include behavioral manifestations). **Oppression** refers to the *act* of putting extreme limitations and constraints on a particular person, group, or larger system.

Discrimination and oppression can both result from stereotypes. **Stereotypes** are schemas about entire groups that contain oversimplified, rigid, and generalized impressions of members of those groups; these impressions are held despite the existence of individual differences among members of the group. A serious consequence of stereotyping is a devaluation of the individual – persons belonging to another group (e.g., another race) are no longer viewed as unique individuals; instead, all members of the group are presumed have the same, often negative or inferior, characteristics.

1. Levels of Racism: Racism has been defined as a system of power and privilege that may be manifested in attitudes, behaviors, and/or institutional structures based on people's skin color (Anderson & Collins, 2004). Jones (2000) identifies three levels of racism:

- *Institutional racism* refers to denial or restriction of material conditions (e.g., access to health care) and access to power to members of minority groups.

- *Personally mediated racism* refers to prejudice and discrimination at the individual level.

- *Internalized racism* refers to "acceptance by members of the stigmatized races of negative messages about their own abilities and intrinsic worth" (p. 1213).

2. Causes of Prejudice and Discrimination: The following are two significant theories that have been developed to explain prejudice and discrimination.

a. Stereotyping: Stereotypes (defined above) exert strong effects on how social information is processed: Information related to an activated stereotype is processed more quickly, people pay closer attention to information that is consistent with their stereotypes, and information that is inconsistent with stereotypes may be denied or actively refuted. Although stereotyping can be viewed as a "natural" process that prevents cognitive overload by reducing large amounts of information to a manageable number of categories, it becomes problematic (i.e., leads to prejudice and discrimination) when traits ascribed to a group are predominantly negative, when the stereotyper is dogmatic and does not accommodate his beliefs to new information, and when the stereotype generates a self-fulfilling prophecy effect.

b. Perceived Threat: Prejudice and discrimination have also been linked to the belief that a particular group represents a direct threat to one's well-being. Sears and colleagues (e.g., Sears, 1988) propose that prejudice and discrimination are currently less blatant than they were in the past and that traditional forms of racism have been largely replaced by **symbolic racism**. (Others refer to this form of racism as "modern racism," "subtle racism," or "aversive racism.") Symbolic racists (a) believe that African-Americans and other minorities threaten or violate such traditional American values as individualism, self-reliance, and the work ethic; (b) deny their prejudices and attribute the social and economic problems of minority group members to internal factors (e.g., lack of effort and discipline); and (c) usually reject obvious forms of prejudice and discrimination, but oppose welfare, affirmative action, and other programs designed to assist those who have been the target of discrimination.

3. Mental Health Consequences of Racial Oppression: Landrum and Batts (1985) address the effects of racial oppression on the mental health of African-Americans and propose that the consequences may take several forms:

- One possible outcome is **internalized oppression**, which can involve system beating (acting out against the system), system blaming, total avoidance of whites, and/or denial of the political significance of race. The latter may be manifested as attempting to earn acceptance by the conspicuous consumption of material goods, using status and educational degrees to elevate one's self-worth, and/or escaping through the use of drugs, food, etc.

- Another response is conceptual incarceration, which involves adopting a white, Anglo-Saxon Protestant worldview and lifestyle.

- A third outcome is the split-self syndrome, which is characterized by polarizing oneself into "good" and "bad" components, with the bad components representing one's African-American identity.

4. Reducing Prejudice and Discrimination: Allport (1954) argues that intergroup prejudice arises from a combination of historical, cultural, economic, cognitive, and personality factors and proposes that, since prejudice has multiple determinants, focusing on only one cause will not lead to a complete understanding or resolution of the problem. He notes, however, that the various causes of prejudice are internalized by the individual and, consequently, that it is the individual who engages in discriminatory practices and who can learn to act in more egalitarian and nondiscriminatory ways. In terms of interventions, Allport asserts that it is not always necessary for "folkways" (personal attitudes and beliefs) to precede "stateways" (legislation), and he proposes that laws prohibiting discrimination can be effective even when they do not reflect public consensus.

Allport was also a supporter of the **contact hypothesis**, which proposes that prejudice may be reduced through contact between members of majority and minority groups as long as the following conditions are met: members of the different groups must have equal status and power; members of the groups should be provided with opportunities that disconfirm their negative stereotypes about members of the other group; contact must be sanctioned by law, custom, and other institutional supports; and contact should require intergroup cooperation to achieve mutual ("superordinate") goals.

B. Culture

1. Acculturation: Acculturation refers to the cultural modification of an individual, group, or people by adapting to or borrowing traits from another culture. It includes the degree to which a member of a culturally diverse group within a society accepts and adheres to the behaviors, values, attitudes, etc., of his own group and the majority group. Contemporary models of acculturation view it as an ongoing process and emphasize that a person can take on the values, attitudes, and behaviors of his new culture without abandoning those of his indigenous culture. According to the **biculturation model**, the best outcome of acculturation is the ability to function well in both cultures (i.e., the ability to alternate effectively between the two cultures).

a. Factors Affecting Acculturation: Factors that can affect acculturation and interactions with the dominant culture include the length of time an immigrant/refugee has lived in the U.S.; his degree of bilingualism; the degree of similarity between his native culture and the dominant culture with respect to behavioral norms, values, beliefs, etc.; the degree of difference between his conceptual style and problem-solving approach and those of the dominant culture; and the degree to which he associates solely or mostly with people who share his cultural background.

b. Acculturation Status: According to Berry and colleagues (1987), **acculturation status** (mode) can be described in terms of four categories:

> *Integration:* The person maintains his own (minority) culture, but also incorporates many aspects of the dominant culture. As noted above, some authors refer to this as a biculturalism.
>
> *Assimilation:* The person accepts the majority culture while relinquishing his own culture.
>
> *Separation:* The person withdraws from the dominant culture and accepts his own culture.
>
> *Marginalization:* The person does not identify with his own culture or with the dominant culture.

Berry further notes that changes related to acculturation can be very stressful for a person, but that the level and consequences of stress are moderated by several factors. For example, in terms of acculturation status, high levels of stress are associated with separation and marginalization, moderate levels are associated with assimilation, and low levels are associated with integration.

c. Intergenerational Conflict: Often, by the third generation, immigrants and refugees have adopted and internalized many of the dominant culture's patterns, although they frequently maintain traditional family relationship patterns. There may, however, be differences in adaptation and acculturation that occur among different family members, with younger members (children, adolescents) adapting much more quickly and rejecting many of their cultural traditions. Such differences in acculturation levels can contribute to family problems and conflict.

2. Racial/Cultural Identity Development Model: Atkinson and colleagues' Racial/Cultural Identity Development Model (1993) distinguishes between five stages that people experience as they attempt to understand themselves in terms of their own culture, the dominant culture, and the oppressive relationship between the two cultures. Each stage reflects changes in how the person views the self, others of the same racial/cultural group, members of other racial/cultural groups, and members of the dominant group.

> *Stage 1 – Conformity:* This stage is characterized by positive attitudes toward and a preference for dominant cultural values and depreciating attitudes toward one's own culture. A client in this stage is likely to prefer a therapist from the majority group.
>
> *Stage 2 – Dissonance:* The dissonance stage is marked by confusion and conflict over the contradictory appreciating and depreciating attitudes that one has toward the self and toward others of the same and different groups. People in this stage are likely to prefer a therapist from a racial/cultural minority group and usually perceive their personal problems as being related to racial/cultural identity issues.
>
> *Stage 3 – Resistance and immersion:* People in this stage actively reject the dominant society and exhibit appreciating attitudes toward the self and toward members of their own group. A person in this stage prefers a therapist from the same racial/cultural group and is likely to perceive personal problems as the result of oppression.
>
> *Stage 4 – Introspection:* This stage is characterized by uncertainty about the rigidity of beliefs held in Stage 3 and conflicts between loyalty and responsibility toward one's group and feelings of personal autonomy. People in this stage continue to prefer therapists from their own group, but are more open to therapists who share a similar worldview.
>
> *Stage 5 – Integrative awareness:* At this stage, people experience a sense of self-fulfillment with regard to their cultural identity and have a strong desire to eliminate all forms of oppression. They also adopt a multicultural perspective and objectively examine the values, beliefs, etc., of their own group and other groups before accepting or rejecting them. In terms of therapist preference, clients in this stage place greater emphasis on similarity in worldview, attitudes, and beliefs than on ethnic, racial, or cultural similarity.

People may progress in a linear way through the five stages, or, because of changes in cross-ethnic/cultural interactions and relationships, may remain at one stage or move forward or backward. In families, members may be at different stages, which can lead to conflicts.

3. Important Cultural Variations:

a. Worldview: As defined by Sue and Sue (2003), **worldview** refers to how a person perceives his relationship to nature, other people, institutions, and so on. These authors argue that it's important to consider worldview in cross-cultural counseling because the worldviews of the therapist and client can affect the therapeutic process.

> *Locus of control and responsibility:* Sue and Sue (2003) maintain that worldview is impacted by a person's cultural background and experiences and is determined by two factors – the person's locus of control and locus of responsibility. For example, white middle-class therapists typically have an internal locus of control and internal locus of responsibility (IC-IR) and, as a result, are likely to misinterpret the behavior of an

African-American client with an external locus of control and external locus of responsibility (EC-ER) as being due to low ego-strength and excessive passivity when, in fact, the client's behavior may actually be a reaction to racial oppression.

Sue and Sue (2003) note that members of minority groups are increasingly likely to exhibit an internal locus of control and external locus of responsibility (IC-ER) as they have become more aware of their own racial and cultural identity and the impact of oppression on their lives. They conclude that this worldview poses the greatest problems for a white therapist with an IC-IR worldview because the client is likely to challenge the therapist's authority and trustworthiness, view the therapist as "part of the Establishment that has oppressed minorities" (p. 285), and be reluctant to self-disclose in therapy.

Individualism vs. collectivism: The worldview known as **individualism** centers on the personal – personal goals, personal uniqueness, and personal control – rather than on the social group or social context in which a person lives. A person with this worldview (a) emphasizes personal self-concept over family life; (b) relates his sense of well-being to a sense of personal control; (c) attributes events or behaviors to dispositional factors; (d) sees events in terms of personal preferences; (e) prefers goal-oriented, direct, low-context communication (see below); and (f) in conflict situations, prefers a confrontational and attributional approach.

The worldview known as **collectivism**, by contrast, assumes that groups connect and mutually obligate individuals – the personal is just one aspect of and is subordinate to the larger social group or context. A person with this worldview (a) emphasizes family life over personal self-concept; (b) does not connect his sense of well-being to a sense of personal control; (c) attributes events or behaviors to situational factors; (d) sees events in terms of what he believes the expectations of others might be; (e) prefers indirect, high-context communication (see below); and (f) in conflict situations, prefers an accommodation and negotiation approach.

b. Communication Patterns: Sue and Sue (2003) describe several aspects of communication that are influenced by culture and may affect interactions between people from different cultural backgrounds: (a) *Paralanguage* refers to the vocal cues (other than language itself) that are used to communicate meaning; (b) *proxemics* refers to the personal and interpersonal use of space; and (c) *kinesics* refers to the use of bodily movements as means of communication.

Nonverbal communication: There are wide variations across cultures with regard to nonverbal communication patterns (e.g., the use and meaning of eye contact, the use and meaning of gestures, and the perception of appropriate personal space). Additionally, many non-white individuals consider nonverbal communication and "reading" people to be as important as verbal communication (i.e., they believe that body language, facial expressions, and nonword sounds can communicate as much as actual speech).

High-context vs. low-context communication (Hall, 1969): With **low-context communication**, information is generally transmitted explicitly and concretely through the language. Low-context communication is less unifying than high-context communication and can change rapidly and easily. Low-context communication is characteristic of Euro-American cultures.

With **high-context communication**, communication is grounded in the situation, depends on group understanding, relies heavily on nonverbal cues, helps unify a culture, and is slow to change. Facial expressions, gestures, and tone of voice are as important as the meaning of words that are said, and stories, proverbs, fables, metaphors, similes, and analogies are often used to make a point. High-context communication is characteristic of many culturally diverse groups in the United States.

In low-context cultures, self-image and self-worth are defined in personal, individual terms (individualism); in high-context cultures, self-image and self-worth are tied to the group (collectivism).

c. Family and Relationship Patterns: Individuals from diverse cultures rely on family and relationship patterns that differ from those typically found among middle-class white Americans. Patterns commonly, although not always, found among African-Americans, American Indians, Asian Americans, and Hispanic/Latino Americans (and, to a lesser degree, lower income white Americans) include the following:

Family patterns: (a) Families are extended (not nuclear). (b) Emphasis is placed on the needs of the family/group (rather than on the needs of the individual). (c) Interdependence and responsibility to the family (rather than independence and autonomy) are emphasized and encouraged. (d) Emphasis is placed on respect for adults and elders (rather on than egalitarian values).

Relationship patterns: (a) Individuals rely on help from family members and use "outside" resources as a last resort. (b) Emphasis is placed on collateral relationships (rather than on individualism). (c) Shame (rather than individual guilt) is used as a tool for controlling interpersonal interactions and other behavior. (d) Individuals distinguish between the public self and private self (rather than striving for an integrated persona).

4. Adaptation of Refugees and Immigrants: Being familiar with the typical adaptation process experienced by immigrants and refugees helps social workers conceptualize the attitudes and behaviors of an immigrant or refugee client.

a. Refugee Process: The **refugee process** outlined below (Gonsalves, 1992) characterizes the common experience of people who move to a new country.

New arrival (1 week to 6 months after arrival): (a) *Events:* Begins learning about the new culture but remains highly involved with the country of origin. (b) *Potential problems/stressors:* Sadness, disorientation, sense of loss, guilt, and low energy (although some new arrivals feel excitement and relief).

Destabilization (6 months to 3 years after arrival): (a) *Events:* Begins to acculturate (often due to economic pressures) and develops survival skills and a support network. May continue to believe that his native country is "better." (b) *Potential problems/stressors:* Stress, loneliness, denial, and angry withdrawal from the new culture, resistance to it, or uncritical conformity to it.

Exploration and restabilization (3 to 5 years after arrival): (a) *Events:* Acquires more flexible ways of learning about the new culture and may prefer contact with other refugees/immigrants and resist further adaptation. (b) *Potential problems/stressors:* Isolation, fear of failure, anger about reduced status, adjustment difficulties, and marital/family conflicts.

Return to normal life (5 to 7 years after arrival): (a) *Events:* Cultural accommodation along with retention of some native cultural values. Forms a positive personal identity, accepts enduring personality changes, and develops realistic expectations for the next generation. (b) *Potential problems/stressors:* Delayed grief reaction and family (especially intergenerational) conflict.

Additionally, at any point after arriving, an immigrant or refugee may experience depression, anxiety, an identity disorder, an existential crisis, psychosomatic complaints, or even psychosis as he struggles to enter the new culture, fulfill survival needs, modify his personal identity, maintain family commitments, and connect his past, present, and future.

For refugees who fled their country of origin because of persecution, war, torture, etc., the escape experience may have included a traumatic event (e.g., rape, assault, forced family separation). PTSD and depression are prevalent in this population, but their symptoms may be masked by substance use disorders in adults or adolescents and by acting out behavior, especially in school, in children and adolescents.

b. Social Displacement Theory: Social displacement theory proposes that Asian immigrants and refugees usually feel happy and optimistic upon arriving in the U.S., but, thereafter, experience a period of depression, confusion, and frustration. Thus, they are likely to display the most severe mental health problems at the end of the first year through the third year after moving to the U.S.

C. Sexual Orientation

The term gay refers to men or to both men and women whose sexual orientation is toward members of the same sex. The term lesbian is used to describe women whose sexual orientation is toward women. The term bisexual is used to describe sexual behavior that is directed to members of the same and opposite sex. The word transgendered refers to a person whose identity differs from conventional expectations for their physical sex. Transgendered people can include transsexuals, drag queens/kings, cross-dressers, and so forth, and transgendered people can be gay, lesbian, bisexual, or straight. Often gay and transgendered people are referred to together as LGBT (lesbian, gay, bisexual, and transgendered) or LGBTQ (with the addition of "questioning"). The word homosexual refers to both gay men and lesbians but is often not the preferred language, as "homosexual" has been associated with negative stereotypes. In the following discussion, we use the term "gay" to refer to both men and women whose sexual orientation is toward members of the same sex.

As a social worker, you should know that the research has shown that it is impossible to reliably differentiate gay people from heterosexuals on the basis of their personality characteristics, family background, gender identity, defenses, ego strengths, object relations, psychopathology, problems in living, or social adjustment (Goldstein, 1997).

1. Homosexual (Gay/Lesbian) Identity Development Model: For each person, the outcome of "homosexual identity formation" is influenced by the presence (or absence) of social supports, positive role models, and satisfying relationships, and by societal attitudes and policies. Troiden's (1988) Homosexual (Gay/Lesbian) Identity Development Model distinguishes between four stages:

Stage 1 – Sensitization, feeling different: During this stage (which is usually characteristic of middle childhood), the individual feels different from his or her peers.

For example, the individual may realize that his or her interests differ from those of same-gender classmates.

Stage 2 – Self-recognition, identity confusion: At the onset of puberty, the individual realizes that he or she is attracted to people of the same sex and attributes those feelings to homosexuality, which leads to turmoil and confusion.

Stage 3 – Identity assumption: During this stage, the individual becomes more certain of his or her homosexuality and may deal with this realization in a variety of ways (e.g., by trying to "pass" as heterosexual, by aligning himself or herself with the gay community, or by acting in ways consistent with society's stereotypes about homosexuality).

Stage 4 – Commitment, identity integration: Individuals in this stage have adopted a homosexual way of life and publicly disclose their homosexuality.

2. Stages of "Coming Out": The stages of coming out have been conceptualized as including those listed below (Coleman, 1985). Not all gay people pass through each stage, however, and, for many people, the process is more complicated and variable than any stage model could show.

Pre-coming out: The person is more or less aware of feelings of same-sex attraction but denies or represses them and may feel alienated (i.e., different from other people), alone, and stigmatized. For some, discovering their sexual orientation produces feelings of loss (e.g., isolation from heterosexual loved ones, suddenly feeling unwelcome in familiar places).

Coming out: The person still feels a great deal of confusion but begins the process of self-acceptance and tolerance. He or she may look for validation from the external environment (other people, the community, etc.).

Exploration: The person feels a growing commitment to his or her gay identity and experiments with new behaviors.

First relationship: The person seeks an intimate same-sex partner.

Integration of identity: This stage is marked by the development of self-acceptance. It often includes a sense of pride about being gay and may include community involvement and political activism.

Although coming out may result in rejection and other negative consequences, it also has beneficial effects. In one study, Jordan and Deluty (1998) found that the more widely lesbians disclosed their sexual orientation to others, the more likely they were to report higher levels of self-esteem and positive affectivity, lower levels of anxiety, and a reduced likelihood of engaging in anonymous socializing (going to gay and lesbian bars to spend time with people they do not know).

3. Homophobia and Related Terms and Concepts:

a. Homophobia: The term homophobia has long been used to refer to an irrational fear or hatred of people oriented toward homosexuality (Barker, 2003). There are three kinds of homophobia: (a) *Individual homophobia* refers to the open hostility and violence demonstrated by individuals toward those who are gay. (b) *Institutional homophobia* refers to overt and covert prejudice found within economic, political, educational, religious, social welfare, and family structures. (c) *Internalized homophobia* refers to the contempt a person has for his or her own actual (or imagined) homosexual orientation (see also Effects of Prejudice and Discrimination, below).

b. Sexual Stigma, Heterosexism, and Sexual Prejudice: Herek (2004) argues that the term homophobia is ambiguous and imprecise and proposes that it be replaced with three terms – i.e., sexual stigma, heterosexism, and sexual prejudice.

- As defined by Herek, *sexual stigma* refers to "the shared knowledge of society's negative regard for any nonheterosexual behavior, identity, relationship, or community" (p. 15). Sexual stigma creates a power and status differential between heterosexuals and homosexuals in which homosexuality is viewed as inferior to heterosexuality.

- *Heterosexism* refers to cultural ideologies, which are "systems that provide the rationale and operating instructions" (p. 15) that promote and perpetrate antipathy, hostility, and violence against homosexuals. Heterosexism includes beliefs about gender, morality, and sexuality that define sexual minorities as deviant or threatening and is inherent in language, laws, and other cultural institutions.

- *Sexual prejudice* refers to negative attitudes that are based on sexual orientation, whether the target is homosexual, bisexual, or heterosexual. Herek notes that, like other attitudes, sexual prejudice does not always accurately predict specific behaviors. However, heterosexual individuals with high levels of prejudice against homosexuals are more likely than those with low levels of prejudice to "respond negatively to gay individuals, support antigay political candidates and policies, and discriminate against gay people" (p. 19).

Herek (2000) notes that research on the correlates of sexual prejudice has generally found higher levels of prejudice among heterosexual men (versus heterosexual women) and among individuals who are older, have lower levels of education, live in Southern or Midwestern states or in rural areas, or have limited personal contact with homosexuals. Other studies have also linked higher levels of sexual prejudice to authoritarianism, affiliation with a fundamentalist religious denomination, and conservative political views.

4. Effects of Prejudice and Discrimination: There is evidence that lesbian, gay, bisexual, and transgender (LGBT) individuals have higher rates of certain psychological problems. For example, as a group, youth who identify as nonheterosexual are more likely than their heterosexual peers to experience depression, anxiety, and substance use and to have a higher risk for suicidality (Cochran & Maya, 2006; Russell, 2006). However, there is also evidence that the increased prevalence of psychological disturbances is not due to sexual orientation itself, but to the prejudice and discrimination that LGBT individuals encounter because of their sexual orientation (e.g., Sue & Sue, 2003).

Social withdrawal and isolation are common responses to stigmatization; and, in one study, Martin and Hetrick (1988) found that social and emotional isolation was the primary presenting problem for a sample of gay adolescents seeking assistance at a social and educational agency for sexual minority youth. Another response is **internalized homophobia**, which occurs when LGBT individuals "accept heterosexual society's negative evaluations of them and incorporate these into their self-concepts" (Renzetti, 1997, p. 290). Consequences of internalized homophobia include low self-esteem, self-doubt or self-hatred, a sense of powerlessness, denial of one's sexual orientation, and self-destructive behavior.

Other consequences of prejudice that are experienced by many LGBT individuals include an ongoing fear that others will discover that they are gay or bisexual, prohibitions against showing affection in public or talking about their partner to others, and exposure to negative media portrayals of LGBT people. And, despite progress, oppressive policies and practices continue to affect the lives of many LGBT people (e.g., discrimination in employment, housing, insurance, inheritance, medical care, marital arrangements, child custody, and adoption proceedings).

D. Gender

1. Gender Roles: Gender encompasses both a person's biological sex and the socially derived expectations about how a person should think, feel, and behave based on his or her biological sex. These expectations, referred to as gender roles, typically begin influencing a person's behavior in early childhood and are influenced by familial, cultural, ethnic, religious, political, and societal factors.

> *Traditional masculinity:* Characteristics of traditional masculinity include independence, assertiveness, ambition, self-confidence, competitiveness, toughness, and anger; having power; and being in control in emotional situations, in sexual relationships, and at work. Males are expected to avoid emotional expressiveness, intimacy, and vulnerability (e.g., weakness, insecurity, worry), which are considered to be "feminine" characteristics.

> *Traditional femininity:* Characteristics of traditional femininity include warmth, dependency, passivity, cooperativeness, and emotional expressiveness; being nurturing and supportive; placing a high priority on one's relationships; and a willingness to tolerate a lower status at work and in marriage. Females are expected to avoid such "masculine" characteristics as competitiveness, assertiveness, and anger.

People who experience a discrepancy between how they believe they should think, feel, or behave based on gender role expectations and how they actually think, feel, or behave experience **gender role conflict**. Both unresolved gender role conflict and adhering to extreme standards of masculinity (for males) or femininity (for females) can have a negative impact on mental health.

2. Effects of Gender/Gender Roles on Stress and Coping:

a. Males:

> *Sources of stress:* Males are likely to experience stress in situations that challenge their view of themselves and cause them to feel inadequate. Those who adhere to traditional standards of masculinity, for example, experience stress when they feel they are not meeting gender role expectations for superior intellect, physical strength, or sexual performance and in situations that require them to express their emotions or be subordinate to women.

> *Responses to stress:* Men typically respond to stress in one or more of the following ways: denying the problem; acting "tough" or as though they are unaffected by the problem; keeping their feelings to themselves; engaging in physical activities that release stress; abusing alcohol or other drugs; or actively attempting to solve or control the problem. Although the research is inconclusive as to whether males or females use problem-solving as a coping strategy more often, problem-solving has been more commonly attributed to

males. As an active coping strategy, problem-solving is more effective than avoidant strategies such as denial or substance abuse.

b. *Females:*

Sources of stress: (a) A significant source of stress for females is the perceived or actual need to occupy and meet the demands of many different social roles at the same time (e.g., wife, mother, homemaker, employee, caregiver to an elderly parent). Meeting the demands of multiple roles simultaneously creates high levels of day-to-day stress, particularly for women who are forced on a regular basis to make difficult choices about their priorities, and can lead to relationship difficulties. Women who believe they have failed to perform or balance all of their roles successfully may experience lowered self-esteem. (b) Both women who choose to work outside the home and those who must do so to support their families usually continue to perform the majority of household duties. In the workplace, women are frequently paid less than men with comparable positions and are often given jobs with less autonomy or creativity, which tends to decrease their level of job satisfaction. (c) Although the ability to form intimate and meaningful relationships helps protect women from the effects of stress, it can also be a source of stress. Females who adhere to traditional notions of femininity may perceive unsuccessful relationships as reflecting a failure on their part to demonstrate expected levels of warmth, nurturance, and empathy. (d) Two additional sources of stress common to women are physical unattractiveness and victimization stemming from the power differential between men and women. Regarding the former, females who adhere to unrealistic standards of feminine beauty and/or who are affected by the double-standard regarding male and female aging are vulnerable to experiencing shame, at risk for developing eating disorders, and may have significant difficulty in accepting the normal physical changes that accompany growing older. Women viewed as unattractive sometimes experience discrimination in the workplace and elsewhere.

Responses to stress: Women usually respond to stress by seeking social support, expressing their feelings, or using distraction. Typical coping strategies include worrying, venting, getting advice, praying, or engaging in behaviors unrelated to the problem (e.g., drinking alcohol). Distraction and seeking social support are ways of relieving the stress associated with a problem rather than ways of resolving or overcoming a problem and are, therefore, considered to be avoidant coping strategies.

3. Gender and Mental Health: Gender influences methods of coping with stress, styles of interacting with others, the expectations of others, self-evaluation, spirituality, and access to resources, which, in turn, impact mental health in positive or negative ways.

Neither males nor females are at higher risk for developing mental disorders per se, but being male or female appears to increase susceptibility to certain types of disorders. Compared to women, men are more likely to experience externalizing disorders such as substance use disorders and antisocial behavior (e.g., anger, hostility, aggression, violence). Substance abuse, in turn, can lead to negative physical and social consequences, including liver and brain damage, divorce, job loss, arrests, and financial debt. Antisocial behavior damages interpersonal relationships. In addition, men who adhere to rigid standards of traditional masculinity by behaving in domineering ways or avoiding emotional expressiveness often have problems in their relationships and are at increased risk for social isolation.

Compared to men, women are more likely to experience internalizing disorders, such as depression and anxiety. Typical symptoms experienced by women include persistent sadness;

a sense of loss, helplessness, or hopelessness; uncertainty about their ability to handle problems; high levels of nervousness or worry; low self-esteem; guilt, self-reproach, and self-blame; decreased energy, motivation, or interest in life; concentration difficulties; and problems with sleep or appetite.

4. Transgender: It is important to understand transgendered individuals and the issues that present for social work on all levels across the lifespan.

Transgender individuals encounter difficulties in many facets of their life lives, both societal pressures for those that do not conform to gender norms to coping with their own feelings of indifference. Verbal harassment to physical violence, possible racial and ethnic discrimination; to even dismissal from jobs and denial of services. Transgender and transsexual people are often denied basic medical and mental health care.

For some transgender individuals, they may experience a discord between their physical body to their internal bodily experience. To help align their physical body with their experience of self, some transgender individuals will seek medical services (e.g., hormone replacement, surgical procedures, etc.). Many medical procedures are often denied coverage, siting reasons as, "experimental" or "cosmetic."

Many transgender children suffer harassment and violence at school, feeling unsafe at school; increasing drop out and suicide. There are still very few support services for transgender children and their parents, leaving them vulnerable and susceptible to "reparative" treatments.

Transgender adults may face barriers to employment, housing, denial of access to civil marriage or domestic partnerships. They are at increased risk of violence and harassment, loss of social support, and over all well-being.

Social workers play a major role in understanding both the oppression and liberation of the transgender community. Social workers are encouraged to understand and challenge the policies at each level when working with transgender individuals. From how they are treated in clinical, health-care, schools, and other institutional settings; to advocating and seeking policy and legal changes to aiding in the quality of life for transgender people.

E. Physical Disability

Individuals with physical disabilities include those with visible or apparent conditions, such as orthopedic or neuromotor impairments, blindness or deafness, or speech disorders, as well as individuals whose physical activity is limited by less apparent chronic conditions such as arthritis, heart disease, high blood pressure, diabetes, or asthma. Some individuals with physical disabilities have lost a range of functioning due to illness or injury, while others never acquired that functioning in the first place.

Williamson (2001) suggests the following definitions for terms commonly used when describing or working with individuals with physical disabilities:

- *Impairment* refers to a restriction in a person's level of physical functioning due to an abnormality or loss of a body part or organ.

- The term *disability* indicates that an impairment has hindered or restricted a person's normal physical functioning. Society tends to function according to the needs of people with typical abilities, which often creates barriers for individuals who have disabilities.

- A *barrier* is a condition created by society that limits a person with a disability from carrying out a normal function (e.g., a person in a wheelchair is unable to enter a building because he cannot climb stairs).

1. Issues Faced by Individuals With Physical Disabilities: Issues frequently faced by individuals with physical disabilities include the following:

- Being more isolated from others than they would like to be.
- A sense of being "different," "damaged," or "useless."
- A greater risk of being abused by others.
- Higher rates of unemployment and poverty.
- Uninformed or negative attitudes toward disability on the part of loved ones or others whom they encounter.
- Discrimination at the institutional level, including difficulties with accessing and using needed services.

In addition, individuals who become physically disabled face multiple losses (e.g., changes in self-image and social status, loss of body parts or functionality) and subsequent grief.

Some individuals with physical disabilities develop a diagnosable depression or related mental disorder as a result of struggling with one or more of the issues listed above. Those diagnosed with a mental disorder and given medication to treat that disorder sometimes find that this medication has a negative impact on their physical disability; in other cases, medication used to manage the individual's physical disability has a negative impact on his mental health.

On the positive side, a significant number of individuals who become physically disabled report undergoing profound spiritual growth as they come to accept their disability and become more consciously aware of and grateful for the positive aspects of their lives, aspects that they took for granted before experiencing the trauma that resulted in their disability.

2. Adaptation to Sudden Physical Disability: Horowitz (1983) has developed a model of adaptation following sudden physical disability that includes the following phases of recovery: shock (emotional "outcry"), denial, intrusive recollections, working through, and completion.

Phase 1 – Shock: Immediately following the trauma that results in disability, the individual experiences a state of shock (emotional "outcry") which leads to a mobilization of his psychological defenses, typically denial or repression.

Phase 2 – Denial: The person may deny the severity of his injury, the prognosis regarding his ultimate level of functionality, the need for surgical interventions, and/or the temporary or permanent impact of the disability on his overall functioning. In this context, denial is adaptive in that it allows the person to avoid experiencing overwhelming emotional pain and to experience and process the trauma in a more gradual way.

Phase 3 – Intrusive recollections: The person begins to recall the trauma through intrusive nightmares or flashbacks in which he relives intense feelings of helplessness, fear, and anxiety. Over time, these recollections can assist the person to re-evaluate and integrate the traumatic experience.

Phase 4 – Working through: The person is faced with the task of grieving his losses and may develop major depression, which is a relatively common reaction following the experience of traumatic disability.

Phase 5 – Completion or the search for meaning: Improved psychological adaptation following trauma is more likely when the person is able to find positive meaning in the traumatic event or its aftermath. In turn, seeking a positive explanation for the trauma is associated with a greater perception of personal control over the disability and its effects. In seeking emotional stability following the trauma, individuals may compare themselves to others who are worse off, re-evaluate the traumatic experience and attempt to learn something valuable from it, or transform the experience by coming to view their suffering as purposeful in some meaningful way.

3. Legislative Acts Protecting Individuals With Physical Disabilities: Legislative acts intended to protect the rights and improve the social interactions of individuals with physical disabilities provide a useful basis for advocacy with and on behalf of clients and others who are disabled.

a. The Rehabilitation Act: The Rehabilitation Act (1973) was passed in an effort to improve employment opportunities for persons with disabling conditions. Key provisions of the Act included access to vocational rehabilitation and other resources to assist these individuals to further their education and training to make them more employable.

b. The Education for All Handicapped Children Act (P.L. 94-142): The Education for All Handicapped Children Act, passed in 1975, mandates that public education must accommodate the unique needs of all children. The law guarantees an appropriate free public education to all children ages 3 to 21 who need special education services, including those with physical disabilities. The law was renamed the **Individuals with Disabilities Education Act**, or IDEA (P.L. 101-476) in 1990. (Additional information on this law appears in the Interventions with Clients/Client System chapter, in the section reviewing school social work.)

c. The EEOC and the Americans With Disabilities Act: The Equal Employment Opportunity Commission (EEOC) is the federal body responsible for enforcing federal laws that make it illegal to discriminate against a job applicant or employee because of the person's disability, genetic information, race, color, religion, gender (including pregnancy), national origin, or age (40 or older).

The **Americans with Disabilities Act** (ADA) of 1990 is a federal law that prohibits discrimination against and ensures equal opportunity for individuals with disabilities in employment. The ADA defines disability as an impairment that substantially limits one or more major life activities, a record of such an impairment, or being regarded as having such an impairment.

- The major areas of discrimination addressed by the ADA include employment, access to public services (e.g., public transportation), access to the goods and services of private accommodations and businesses, and overcoming barriers to information in telecommunications (e.g., telephone, televised programming).

- Under this law, a "qualified person with a disability" is someone with a disability who, with or without reasonable accommodation, can perform the essential functions of the job he holds or has applied for.
- **Reasonable accommodation** involves, among other things, making existing workplace facilities readily accessible to and usable by the person with a disability and the acquisition or modification of equipment.
- Workplace discrimination under the ADA includes either (a) not making reasonable accommodation to the limitations of an otherwise qualified person with a disability, unless the employer can show that the accommodation would impose an undue hardship on the operation of his business; or (b) denying a job opportunity to someone who is an otherwise qualified person with a disability if this denial is based on the need to make reasonable accommodation to overcome his limitations.

The ADA Amendments Act of 2008 (P.L. 110-325) made changes to the definition of the term "disability" in the ADA to make it easier for an individual seeking protection under the ADA to establish that he has a disability within the meaning of the ADA. Although the Act retains the ADA's basic definition of "disability" (see above), it changes the way terminology contained in the definition should be interpreted by the EEOC. In particular, the EEOC was required to revise its regulations defining "substantially limits" and to expand its definition of "major life activities." For instance, an impairment that is episodic or in remission is now considered a disability if it substantially limits a major life activity when active; and the definition of "major life activities" now includes two non-exhaustive lists covering (a) many activities that the EEOC recognized before (e.g., walking) as well as activities that EEOC had not specifically recognized (e.g., reading, bending, communicating); and (b) major bodily functions (e.g., functions of the immune system, normal cell growth, digestive, bowel, bladder, neurological, brain, respiratory, circulatory, endocrine, and reproductive functions).

F. Poverty and Homelessness

Poverty

1. Definition and Types of Poverty: Barker (2003) defines poverty as "the state of being poor or deficient in money or means of subsistence." The term **poverty line** refers to a measure of the amount of money that the government, or a society, believes is necessary for a person to live at a minimum level of subsistence (Barker, 2003). The term **subsistence level** refers to the lowest amount of money or resources needed to survive.

Types of poverty include:

- *Absolute poverty* – below a subsistence level of income.
- *Relative poverty* – below the standard of living of one's mainstream community.

In addition, people who are impoverished may be described as either transitional poor, marginal poor, or residual poor:

- *Transitional poor* – a person is briefly and temporarily impoverished as a result of a specific event in his life or environment.
- *Marginal poor* – a person moves in and out of poverty because of job insecurity, inadequate skills, and/or limited education.

- *Residual poor* – the poverty is long-term and intergenerational.

2. The "Underclass": The system of social class stratification divides people into categories based on socioeconomic factors, including income and education (e.g., lower class, middle class, upper class). Some people, such as economists, use the term "underclass" to refer to the poorest of the poor – to people considered "trapped" by social and economic factors such as discrimination, lack of education, and lack of marketable job skills, and by personal factors such as chronic mental illness. This group is comprised disproportionately of people of color and is one of the most oppressed groups in U.S. society. Additionally, feeling alienated from one's community and lacking hope for the future are common characteristics of people who live in areas where economic conditions are poor (such as inner-cities), and people experiencing these feelings are often members of the "underclass."

A related term is "culture of poverty," which refers to the prejudicial belief held by some in society that poor people are impoverished because their values, norms, and motivations prevent them from taking advantage of opportunities available to achieve economic independence (Barker, 2003).

3. Economic Deprivation: Economic deprivation is present when a person (or group) has inadequate or unjustly limited access to financial resources. This can result from unemployment, job discrimination, insufficient work benefits, harmful public policies, etc.

4. Children Living in Poverty: Children living in poverty are exposed to a range of problems that place them at risk for biophysical, psychological, and social difficulties. Examples include poor nutrition, lack of health insurance, inadequate or inconsistent caregiving, and exposure to higher-than-average levels of violence, family separation, and family disruption. In addition, the availability and quality of social resources tend to be lower in impoverished communities.

Although the negative effects of living in poverty can have long-term consequences for children, these consequences can be counteracted by **early intervention programs** designed to help infants at risk due to socioeconomic factors. At-risk infants involved in early intervention between birth and 3 years of age have been found to exhibit improved cognitive development and social competence (Ramey & Ramey, 1998), and these benefits appear to be long-lasting. Also, a number of federally funded programs are available to address the risks faced by children living in poverty. Examples include WIC, Medicaid, TANF, and project Head Start. (See Section VI of Interventions with Clients/Client Systems and the Glossary provided with these materials for more information on these programs.)

Homelessness

In the United States, most of the homeless are people with disabilities or chronic physical or mental illness who lack support for housing, older people on fixed incomes who lack family support, war veterans, undocumented and documented immigrants, former prisoners who had inadequate support for their return to society, and employed and unemployed people who lack adequate income to afford housing (Hopper, 2003). At any given time, about one-third of the homeless population consists of families with children.

1. Factors Contributing to Homelessness: Some people become homeless following a series of crises, poor decision-making, and/or missed opportunities. Other significant contributing factors include alcohol and drug abuse, deinstitutionalization of the mentally ill (see below), joblessness, the need to flee from abuse at home, reduced welfare benefits, and a lack of family support (Ashford et al., 2006). Additionally, as the number of employed and unemployed poor has increased in the nation, the availability of low-income housing has decreased. Thus, some people become homeless due to a combination of poverty and a lack of available low-cost housing.

2. Mental Illness and Homelessness: It has been estimated that around 20 to 25 percent of the single, adult, homeless population suffers from a severe, persistent mental illness (e.g., bipolar disorder, schizophrenia, drug addiction). Many of these individuals are unaware of how state and federal support systems work and how to claim benefits and entitlements, which increases their chances of remaining homeless and isolated from family and friends.

Reasons why people with serious mental illness may become homeless include inadequacies in the mental-health care system, the disabling effects of an untreated mental illness, the combined effects of alcoholism or drug abuse and mental illness, an inability to set realistic life goals, loss of an adequate income due to mental illness, and diminished social supports (Ashford et al., 2006). In turn, many of these problems are related to the effects of deinstitutionalization.

3. Deinstitutionalization: The policy of deinstitutionalization is based on the premise that a community should be responsible for the mental health of its citizens. Examples of how deinstitutionalization has been implemented in communities include the establishment of halfway houses (which are designed to facilitate the transition of patients with mental illness from psychiatric hospitals to the community) and the funding of community mental-health centers (which were created to provide community care so that people with mental illness would no longer have to live in psychiatric hospitals). Ideally, efforts are made to provide patients who have who mental illness with adequate programs both before and subsequent to their release from a hospital. As noted above, however, the policy of deinstitutionalization has proven to be a contributing factor to homelessness among the mentally ill, and one reason for this is that many people with mental illness do not receive adequate **discharge planning** and are released from hospitals without adequate provision for aftercare or follow-up treatment in their community.

4. McKinney Act: The McKinney Act (1987) was the first federal response to homelessness. The original act consisted of 15 programs that provided various services including transitional housing, emergency shelter, job training, primary health care, education, and some permanent housing.

5. Programs for People Who are Homeless: Although some research shows that individuals who are homeless come to accept their way of life, other studies have found that, when programs are available, homeless people will use them. Examples of interventions and services that have been effective for individuals who are homeless include outreach, early engagement in treatment, case management, supported housing (e.g., transitional living programs, Section 8 SRO housing), tailoring treatment plans to individual needs, and providing access to therapy and opportunities to engage in meaningful daily activities. (For more information on Section 8 SRO housing, see the Glossary provided with these materials.)

Finally, studies show that homeless individuals with mental illness and those with addictive disorders share similar treatment needs, including an emphasis on initial engagement in treatment, case management, housing options, and long-term follow-up and support services.

6. Homeless/Runaway Youth: Runaway youth include children who are gone from their homes either because they have run away or because they have been thrown out by their caregivers. Many youth who have left home were physically or sexually abused at home in the year prior to running away.

Drug and alcohol abuse, isolation, feelings of hopelessness, and thoughts of suicide are common among youth who are homeless. In addition, homeless youth are at extremely high risk for victimization (e.g., robbery, rape, assault), exposure to HIV and other STDs, and involvement in illegal activities (e.g., prostitution, drug sales); and very few of them know how to access the resources they need to address the social and health problems they face.

G. Criminal Justice Systems

Criminal justice social work is a field of forensic social work which incorporates social work practice into the legal system, including both civil and criminal law. While there has been a decline in the number of adults in correctional facilities since 2012, there is still almost 7 million people in the United States involved in the justice system. Criminal activity is often associated with chronic poverty, substance abuse, mental illness, and lack of impulse control; while many involved in the justice system are persons of color and lower socioeconomic status.

Social workers in this field of practice may encounter various positions including, adult and juvenile corrections, community-based probation and parole agencies, mental health facilities, public defender's offices, family court agencies, etc. While social workers have been involved within the criminal justice system since the 1800s, the amount of current social workers that identify criminal justice social work as a primary area of focus, is relatively small.

Due to the significant turnover in prisons, the number of prisoners returning to the community upon competition of their sentence is increasing. Two crucial factors of concern are re-arrest rates and the rate of increase of women prisoners versus men. The rate of incarceration of women has increased almost twice as fast as the rate for men (Berg-Weger, 2016). In helping to address these issues, social workers should focus on advocacy and evidence biopsychosocial services that emphasize rehabilitation. The NASW calls for social workers to be trained in working with those connected to the criminal justice system and focus on developing intervention plans to help this population.

VIII. Social Policy

"Policies" are written rules that have been ratified by a legitimate authority and define what actions are allowable and what actions are prohibited. "**Social policy**" includes the "[A]ctivities and principles of a society that guide how it intervenes in and regulates the relationships among individuals, groups, communities, and social institutions. These principles and activities are the result of the society's values and customs and largely determine the distribution of resources and level of well-being of its people. Thus, social policy includes plans and programs in education, health care, crime and corrections, economic security, and social welfare made by governments, voluntary organizations, and the people in general. It also includes social perspectives that result in society's rewards and constraints" (Barker, 2003, p. 405). Social policies that are influenced by a **collectivism** (common good) perspective assume that some individual choice must be limited to better serve the common good. In contrast, social policies leaning toward **individualism** try to place few restrictions on personal freedom and individual will.

A. Evolution of Social Service Delivery in the U.S.

1. Early Efforts to Address Social Problems: In the 1870s, charity organization societies (COS) were introduced to address the problems of immigrants and individuals moving into industrialized cities in search of jobs. The philosophy underlying the work of COS agencies was influenced, in part, by Social Darwinism, an ideology that assumes that income differences between the wealthy and poor exist because the wealthy are naturally "more fit." As a result, COS assistance was generally targeted toward people deemed capable of becoming members of the industrial workforce, and COS volunteers directed their efforts toward changing individuals (i.e., helping the poor overcome their "personal deficits") rather than changing systems (Chambers, 1985). At around the same time, in the late 1800s, settlement houses were established to address dire conditions in slums and tenement houses in industrialized cities. In contrast to COS volunteers, settlement house workers emphasized both individual reform and societal change. These early efforts to address social problems ultimately demonstrated the need for a more systematic approach to helping the poor and for formal training on how to bring about social change. The establishment of American schools of social work followed shortly thereafter in response to those needs.

2. The Trend Toward Centralization: Until the 1800s, efforts to help the poor in the U.S. were mostly local and small in scale (i.e., they were decentralized). The *reformist movement* of the early 19th century initiated a gradual shift to larger-scale services by establishing state-run asylums for individuals with mental illness and others in need of intensive ongoing care. Additional public and private programs were created as the nation's population grew, more people moved into cities, and service needs increased, and, over time, it became clear that these programs needed to be coordinated. By the mid-1890s, many states had established State Boards of Charities, which marked the beginning of state governments' active involvement in the *centralized* coordination of social welfare services. The next major effort toward establishing greater public agency involvement in social welfare services occurred during the *progressive movement* in the early 1900s, when, for example, the first state public welfare department was created.

The *New Deal programs* created during the Great Depression produced the nation's first large, governmental human service agencies. Because a key function of those agencies was to distribute relief funds to states, the New Deal programs also encouraged the opening of additional state public welfare departments. With the creation of the Department of Health, Education, and Welfare (now called the Department of Health and Human Services) in 1956, a number of federal agencies were combined into a cabinet-level organization through which federal social welfare programs are administered.

3. The Social Security Act: Events underlying the Great Depression demonstrated that people could be poor as the result of societal dysfunction, and this realization prompted the development of relief programs including New Deal programs and programs of the Social Security Act.

The Social Security Act (1935) is federal legislation designed to help meet the economic needs of older people, dependent survivors, people with disabilities, and low-income families. The two major provisions of the Act, in its original form, were (a) a mandatory insurance program for workers funded by payroll taxes (FICA) and matching employer contributions, and (b) a public assistance program financed by federal and state treasuries.

The term "public assistance" refers to federal, state, or local programs by which the government provides financial assistance to individuals or families with no other means of supporting themselves. See Section VI in Interventions with Clients/Client Systems for descriptions of specific social security programs (i.e., examples of present-day programs include TANF and Supplemental Security Income, or SSI).

The Social Security Act has been amended several times since its inception. For example, under Title XX (1974), states started receiving funding for social service programs through "block grants" from the federal government. This amendment was designed, in part, to increase the self-reliance of individuals living in poverty with the goal of preventing, reducing, or eliminating dependency on welfare, and to change the way social services are delivered to low-income people, in particular to provide services in a more economical manner. Title XX is also known as the Social Services Block Grant (SSBG). Another amendment, Title XIX (1965), established what is now known as Medicaid. (Note: "Block grant" is a system of disbursing funds that permits the recipient to determine how best to distribute the money.)

4. Welfare Reform – PRWORA: The Personal Responsibility and Work Opportunity Reconciliation Act (PRWORA), passed in 1996, was designed to reform the nation's welfare system and has resulted in significant changes to public assistance programs. A fundamental goal of PRWORA was to change the welfare system into one that requires work in exchange for time-limited assistance. To this end, the law requires "able-bodied" recipients (with a few exceptions) to work after no more than two years on cash assistance. In addition, families receiving assistance for five cumulative years may become ineligible for cash aid (the law allows states to exempt up to 20 percent of their caseload from this provision).

PRWORA's direct impact on public assistance programs was significant. The law either eliminated or placed new restrictions on eight national programs including AFDC, the Food Stamp program, Social Services Block Grants, child protection programs, child nutrition programs, Medicaid, and the earned income tax credit (EITC). PRWORA established

Temporary Assistance to Needy Families (TANF), which replaced AFDC, the Job Opportunities and Basic Skills Training (JOBS) program, emergency assistance, and some provisions in Medicaid, SSI, and other programs. (See Section VI of Direct and Indirect Practice for a description of TANF.) Finally, PRWORA also simplified the legal process for paternity establishment and instituted child support enforcement measures intended to increase child support collections and reduce federal welfare costs.

5. The Patient Protection and Affordable Care Act: The Patient Protection and Affordable Care Act (PPACA), passed in 2010, is also known as the Affordable Care Act (ACA) or "ObamaCare." The major goals of the ACA are to provide better access to affordable, quality health insurance and reduce the growth in health-care spending. In its original form, the ACA was designed to expand health-care coverage in three major ways:

State health exchanges: These are marketplaces where individuals and small businesses (up to 100 employees) can compare and purchase insurance plans.

Expansion of Medicaid coverage: The original ACA required states to extend Medicaid eligibility to a wider pool of low-income individuals and families (i.e., those with income up to 138 percent of the federal poverty line) and provided states with additional funding to do so. This requirement was found to be unconstitutional by the Supreme Court, however, on the grounds that it imposed an unfair burden on states. As a result of this ruling, states now determine for themselves whether to participate in the Medicaid expansion.

Expansion of Medicare coverage: The ACA added free preventive care benefits (annual wellness visits, mammograms) and improved prescription benefits to make medications more affordable for most seniors (i.e., the ACA will gradually close what has been known as the "doughnut hole," a coverage gap in Medicare Part D that forced beneficiaries to pay 100 percent of their prescription drug costs up to a certain amount).

B. Policies Affecting Social Service Delivery

The term "eligibility" refers to both (a) the criteria used by a social service or social welfare program to determine which people may receive the help it offers; and (b) the meeting of pre-determined qualifications to receive certain benefits (Barker, 2003).

1. Major Eligibility Policies: Social welfare policy includes laws and regulations that determine who qualifies for (i.e., is eligible for) a program's services or benefits:

- With the policy known as *exceptional eligibility*, services or benefits are developed for individuals in a special group (such as war veterans), usually due to sympathy for the group or political pressure. Eligibility is not necessarily based on need or circumstances.

- With *selective eligibility*, services or benefits are provided only to individuals who meet pre-established criteria. The amount of the benefit varies based on special needs, circumstances, or economic status. See also Means Testing below.

- With *universal eligibility*, services or benefits are provided in the same amount to all individuals in the nation, rather than on the basis of need, circumstance, or economic status. When applied, this policy can take the form of *universal programs*, such as OASDI (Social Security) and Medicare. Universal programs are open to everyone who falls into a specified category – individuals in that category are not required to undergo tests of need or income. (A synonymous term is "entitlement program" – entitlement programs are government-sponsored benefits of cash, goods, or services that are due to all people who belong to specific class. Examples include OASDI and Medicare.)

2. Means Testing: Means testing is a process used to evaluate a person's financial means or well-being based on variables such as his income, debts, health, and number of dependents. The results are used to determine the person's eligibility to receive a benefit – if the person has the "means" to pay for the services he is seeking, he will be turned down. Federal programs and services that use means testing (e.g., TANF, the Food Stamp Program, and Medicaid) help low-income people by providing cash and noncash benefits. They are provided to individuals and families whose income falls below predefined levels and who meet certain other eligibility criteria established for each program.

3. The Categorically Needy and Categorical Programs: "Categorically needy" individuals are those who are automatically eligible for certain welfare benefits, without a means tests, because they fit some predetermined criteria. In turn, "categorical programs" provide social services and other benefits to people who belong to specifically designated groups that are particularly at risk, such as older people, children without parents, and people who are blind or disabled (Barker, 2003). The term "categorical assistance," in turn, describes welfare programs for specific groups of people identified in the Social Security Act. The federal Supplemental Security Income (SSI) program is an example of a categorical program.